LAKELAND ROCK

LAKELAND ROCK

Classic Climbs
with Chris Bonington

Adrian Bailey

Weidenfeld and Nicolson · London

Acknowledgements

Many people have generously assisted me in the production of this book, by providing technical knowledge, photographs from private collections, personal reminiscences, and valuable criticism. In addition to the principal climbers featured herein, all who have given freely of their time and kept their patience, I would like to thank Shirley Angell and Jay Turner of the Pinnacle Club; Muriel Files of the Fell and Rock Climbing Club of the English Lake District; Nat Allen of the Rock and Ice Club; Mo Anthoine; Dave Armstrong; Pete Botterill; Joe Brown; David Durrans of Kodak; John Sheard, and finally all those in Border Television who supplied research material, guided me through the Lake District, and politely looked away when I slipped on the scree . . .
Adrian Bailey

The author and publisher are grateful to the following for supplying and authorizing reproduction of the illustrations:

(The letters at the end of each caption indicate the source of the photographs.)

(AB)	Adrian Bailey (courtesy Kodak)	(DE)	Daily Express
		(PB)	Paul Berriff
(BT)	Border Television	(BP)	Bill Peascod
(CB)	Chris Bonington	(BB)	Bert Beck
(JS)	John Sheard	(ABK)	Abrahams Bros. Keswick
(PL)	Pete Livesey		
(F & RCC)	Fell and Rock Climbing Club	(LSCC)	Ladies Scottish Climbing Club
(PM)	Pat Morrow	(PC)	The Pinnacle Club
(ICL)	Images Colour Library		

Jacket/cover: The photograph of Pete Whillance on the front is by Chris Bonington. The photograph of Chris Bonington on the back is by Adrian Bailey.

Frontispiece: Chris Bonington on 'Extol', one of the classic hard climbs of the English Lake District. (CB)

Published in Great Britain
by George Weidenfeld & Nicolson Limited 91 Clapham High Street
London SW4 7TA

ISBN 0 297 78637 7 Cased
ISBN 0 297 78638 5 Paperback

Printed and bound in Great Britain by
Butler & Tanner Ltd, Frome and London

Contents

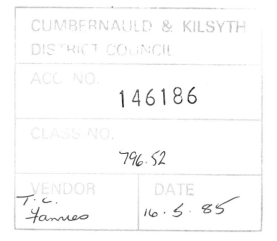

Introduction by Chris Bonington

Rock climbing, like any sport or human activity, is in a constant state of evolution, each generation of climbers trying to surpass the efforts of its predecessors. Within this evolution there are two conflicting trends: the desire for adventure, which is all about risk and the unknown, and the instincts of self-preservation combined with an ambition to achieve success. The former instinct takes the climber onto new untouched stretches of rock which of necessity must be ever steeper, with smaller and smaller holds, as all the easier lines are explored. The climber is therefore pushing himself to extend the limits of what is possible. But to to do this he has to develop better equipment both to surmount increasingly difficult obstacles and to do so with a margin of safety.

In this respect the purest form of adventure is that of the solo climber, the person who goes by himself, without the safeguard of a rope, with his life literally in his hands. Most of us, however, prefer to hedge our bets with some kind of safety net, using a rope and a series of running belays to reduce the danger.

It is the conflict between these two opposing pressures that creates the continual arguments amongst climbers about what is fair and ethical. It is never possible to say precisely what the balance should be between the search for adventure and the need for a degree of safety.

In the series of five programmes that I was asked by Border Television to devise for Channel 4, I wanted to explore the development of climbing over the last fifty years through the memories of leading climbers who had been major pioneers of Lakeland routes. In the series I wanted to portray not just the climbing in isolation but also the changes in social conditions over this period and the richness and variety of the personalities that you meet on the climbing scene.

Fifty years ago the techniques and paraphernalia of climbing had not developed much beyond those used by the pioneers of the nineteenth century. The climber had a hemp rope and perhaps a single loop or sling of hemp with a steel karabiner or snaplink to use as a running belay. In effect the leader could not afford to fall off and if he did the consequences were likely to be fatal.

In the span of my own climbing career, which started in 1951, I have seen modern climbing techniques evolve from the very simplest to the highly sophisticated. My first pair of boots were nailed with clinkers that looked like knobbly molar teeth and were made of a soft iron. My first rope was made of hemp. It dated from before the war and was so worn that I was worried whether it would hold the weight of a second man, let alone that of a falling leader. I found, therefore, that I could fully empathise with the climbers of earlier generations. Indeed, there are a few, now in their sixties, who are still climbing actively.

To portray the development of climbing over the last fifty years, I decided to choose one first ascent from each decade, which was representative of the climbing standards of the time, and then to re–enact that ascent with at least one of the original participants, ideally using the same kind of gear that was used at the time of the first ascent. In doing this we would be able to capture not only the flavour of the original ascent but also the atmosphere of the period.

The first programme was to represent the forties but, in effect, was typical of all pre-Second World War climbing. The climb was Eagle Front, high in Burtness Comb above Buttermere. It was first climbed by Bill Peascod, a young West Cumbrian miner, in 1940. He is now sixty-four, loves climbing as much as ever, and led me up the route he had pioneered forty four years earlier. What was more, it rained throughout most of the week that we were filming the climb and as a result the rock was wet and greasy. We started out with the hawser-like hemp rope that Bill had originally used but in view of the conditions felt justified in changing over to modern gear after the first pitch. Even so we had to climb with socks over our rubber soled shoes to gain some grip on the greasy rock. Leading the entire climb

was a remarkable achievement for a man of Bill's age.

The climb I chose to represent the fifties was Dove Dale Groove, a steep and uncompromising line on Dove Crag on the Eastern Fells. It was first climbed by Joe Brown and Don Whillans, the two young plumbers who dominated British climbing throughout the decade. Dove Dale Groove was a characteristically bold line and it was ten years before it was repeated. They did most of their pioneering in the Peak district and North Wales but they made the occasional foray into the Lake District.

The advance in climbing standards was in some degree the result of improvements in equipment. The war had brought about the introduction of nylon rope and slings which were more elastic and therefore very much stronger than hemp. The use of thin nylon line slings meant that more of them could be carried and they could be placed behind tiny rocky flakes. In addition, Brown and Whillans perfected the art of inserting small pebbles, gathered at the foot of the climb, into cracks and threading their slings behind them. This meant that while Bill Peascod's generation would have climbed with, at the most one, or perhaps two, running belays to protect them on a pitch, the generation of the fifties might have several. None the less, compared to modern gear their protection was inadequate.

I had done some of the best climbing of my life with Don in the late fifties and early sixties, with the first British ascents of the South West Pillar of the Dru in 1958, the Central Pillar of Freney in 1961 and the Central Tower of Paine in South Patagonia in 1963. Of all my climbing partners, Don had the finest mountain judgment. As so often happens, through differences in personality and the pressures of success, we had drifted apart and this was the first time we had been on a rope together for fourteen years. It was something that I think Don, as well as I, appreciated and this came across in the warmth and humour that filled the programme.

It was in the 1960's that I started living in the Lake District and it was in this period that I did most of my first ascents there. I could never claim to be a major Lakeland pioneer, though I did manage to pick off one or two very attractive plums. The two outstanding Lakeland climbers of this period were Alan Austin, for the sheer number of his new routes, and Les Brown, for the quality and selectivity of the comparatively few climbs he put up over this period. Yet the actual climbs were only marginally harder than those pioneered by Whillans and Brown. Back in Wales Brown teamed up with Peter Crew in the mid-sixties to put up some of the hardest climbs being pioneered at that time, while in 1960, in the Lake District, Whillans led Extol, breaching the great blank wall to the right of Dove Dale Groove. This was to be one of the hardest and certainly most serious routes in the Lake District well into the late sixties.

Climbing equipment improved considerably. The special climbing shoe, the PA, had been introduced into Britain in the mid fifties. PAs had a much better grip than ordinary gym shoes and also gave the feet much greater support enabling the climber to use small holds with confidence. The most important development of all, though, was the 'nut' – (as in nuts and bolts). I first used 'nuts' in 1964, but I believe they had been used by a few discerning and technically minded climbers from the late fifties. Threaded onto a sling, their threads drilled out, they could be slotted into cracks very much more quickly and easily than any chock stone.

I chose the Holy Ghost as the representative climb of the sixties mainly because it gave a good story in which I was directly involved. Our ascent had started as a grand project to make a new and demanding traverse of the East Buttress of Scafell but after thoroughly frightening myself on the second pitch we escaped upwards to complete a climb that was probably as hard and serious as anything that had been climbed in the Lakes in 1965, but which, none the less, gave a fairly uninspiring line. A few years later Colin Read and John Adams finished what we had started, climbing the Lord of the Rings, a route that must rank as the finest girdle traverse in the United Kingdom.

The seventies brought the next major breakthrough in climbing standards. Although there were major improvements in the design of equipment, particularly in the development of ranges of wedge – shaped 'nuts' that could be fitted into the smallest cracks, it was a fresh state of mind that was the real reason for the advance. Although climbers had trained sporadically on boulders and even in the gym since the earliest days of the sport, an intense training schedule had never been followed in a systematic way. It was Pete Livesey who brought an athletic approach to climbing. As a schoolboy, he had been in the British athletics squad, had then taken up pot-holing and had only come to serious, high standard climbing at the comparatively late age of thirty.

Training intensively on a local climbing wall he was able to push his standard well beyond that of his peers and put up a series of new routes in the early seventies that were several grades beyond what had previously been completed. He demonstrated that it was ability rather than technical equipment that mattered by making several of his major first ascents, solo.

Footless Crow, on Goat Crag, Borrowdale, was probably his finest new route in the Lakes. It follows a line up an almost continuously overhanging wall which had originally been climbed entirely by artificial means. This climb was made by the local Borrowdale pioneer, Paul Ross. At the time of this aided first ascent, there wasn't any criticism at all, it being inconceivable that such rock could be climbed free. Pete Livesey made his ascent in a single incredible run out of over a hundred and fifty feet, finishing the climb by letting his second man untie the rope so that in effect he was climbing the last thirty feet or so, solo.

I had considerable reservations about trying to follow Livesey up this climb since at a standard of E5 it was a couple of grades harder than anything I had ever managed to climb. I was forewarned of Livesey's genius for gamesmanship by an article in the magazine *Crags*, in which John Sheard, one of his closest friends, described his running commentary during a climbing film they were taking part in: 'He likes the rope tight, so I'll give the bugger a load of slack.' I knew what to expect.

Just to make sure I didn't make a total fool of myself, I cheated and climbed the route a few days before with Pete Whillance. Now Whillance is a gentleman. He put the runners in just the right places to give me the maximum assistance on the crux, told me how to get the most help from the rope and when I started climbing I never once had to call for a tight rope – it was as taut as a bow string all the way up.

With Livesey it was very different. Every time I screamed "Tight", the rope would give a couple of inches and at the same time, for the benefit of the microphone at his throat, Livesey would croon, 'I'm pulling as hard as I can, do you want me to call for a winch?'

Eventually I ran out of strength and spun out into space. It was just as well I had brought a pair of jumar clamps with me and was able to climb up the rope. At least it showed just how hard modern climbing can be. I also had had the satisfaction of seeing Livesey having three controlled falls on the crux, whilst I had given him a super tight rope from the top running belay to help him across the difficult section.

From the earliest days of climbing women have taken part in the sport, though they have always been a minority and there has also been a gap between their leading standard and that of male climbers. In recent years women have undoubtedly been narrowing the gap, leading into the upper extreme grades. Jill Lawrence and Gill Price climbed 'Empire' which is graded E3 and is certainly the most difficult climb that any British woman has ever led in front of the cameras. Before this women have always been shown in their traditional role as seconds on the rope.

The generation of the eighties has taken training a step beyond the levels introduced by Livesey and equipment technology has also improved with the introduction of the 'Friend', a camming

9

device, the 'Rock', a curved wedge–shaped nut, and sticky rubber climbing shoes. As a result standards have continued to rise and climbs like Footless Crow are now well down the list of difficulty. 'Barely rates an E5 grading', commented Pete Whillance as he set out to make the first ascent of Incantations on Napes Crag, the climb he chose and put up specially as his contribution for the TV programme, representing the state of the art today. Not only are the two cruxes of the climb overhanging, but the holds are small and awkwardly placed.

The difficulties of these modern routes are so great that a prior inspection on a rope, when the rock can be cleaned with a wire brush and runner placements can be investigated, is common practice. On the overhanging head wall that formed the final barrier to Incantations, there were no good nut placements and so they hammered in a piton while inspecting the climb on a rope. A few years ago this would have been considered cheating but ethics are for ever changing. The standard of climbing has become so high that the leader is pushing himself to the point where it is inevitable he has frequent falls. If he wants to remain alive and uninjured he must ensure that his running belays are going to stop him hitting the deck. On the top pitch of Incantations, Pete would have hit the steep slab below if he had fallen and would almost certainly have injured himself badly. The piton, therefore, was an insurance, but even so its placement, as with so many modern routes, raised the inevitable question of whether he should

not have left the pitch to someone who was prepared to dare all. Anyway, it was a magnificent piece of climbing and I have a feeling it will be a long time before anyone leads it without the security of that piton.

Putting the five programmes together was both hard work and a lot of fun. I was able to renew old friendships, build new ones and gain a perspective of climbing attitudes and techniques as they have developed over a period of forty years. Although the approach and techniques used by Peascod and Whillans were very different from those employed by Livesey or Whillance, they all have the same rugged individualism, competitive drive and love of climbing. The modern climber has been forced to a greater level of dedication and training by the inevitably rising standards as every bit of unclimbed rock is explored.

The essential principles of the sport remain the same: a drive to explore the limits of human capability in terms of risk and physical ability and yet, at the same time, to have some kind of safety net in the shape of effective running belays and also a reasonable chance of success. Looking into the future it is difficult to predict what climbers will be doing in another forty years time but I have a feeling that the equation between the need to play a danger game and yet maintain a level of safety, the desire for the unknown combined with the urge for success, will remain much the same. The beauty of the Lakeland Hills, I hope, will never change.

Chris Bonington.

1

Pillar Rock

Climbing rocks, especially in perilous circumstances, provides a source of pleasure for a steadily increasing number of people: 'It is difficult to tell at what stage we ceased to look upon the climb as a lark and recognised it as a serious struggle with the issue no foregone conclusion. We had no watches, but by the time we reached the Amphitheatre we seemed to have been climbing for hours up endless ice walls. The lake, framed between the retaining walls, seemed a very long way down, but we knew that we still had a long way to go. We were tired, soaked through and through and half-frozen. We tried to wring some of the water out of our clothes and laughed at the squelching sound in our boots as we walked.' The climbers were E. Banner Mendus and Bill Peascod, ascending the Great Gully of Wastwater Screes in the Lake District in 1944, and loving every minute of it, for they were following in the great tradition of Lakeland climbing. Had not the legendary O.G. Jones – 'the Only Genuine Jones' – whipped off his Norfolk jacket and kicked off his boots in order to climb Walker's Gully in spite of the fact that 'a solid jet of ice-cold water was shooting straight down the middle?' This was a first ascent, in 1899, but surely Jones didn't have to do it in *January*, so that he and his two companions were made 'supremely uncomfortable?' Was he mad? Perhaps the early Victorian pioneer Alpinist, Professor J. Tyndall, had started the fashion, walking on Helvellyn in an advancing storm where 'there was something sugges- tive of madness in the demeanour of the wind – a wild unreasoning fury, like that of a woman with strong feelings, and little intellect to guard them.'

The Lake District of Cumbria owes its uniquely unpredictable pattern of weather to the proximity of the sea, and to the prevailing western winds that carry a moisture-laden atmosphere to the high peaks of the Cumbrian mountains. Cumbria has the distinction of being the wettest place in Britain, and there's a local saying that goes: 'If you can see Cross Fell it's going to rain, and if you can't it's raining.' Never mind – the damp climate is a factor to the advantage of the region's great natural beauty where 'moss runs unbroken to the sky' and the moisture bestows a delicate, blue softness to the landscape. At certain times of the year, especially towards winter, the atmospheric conditions can create apocalyptic sunsets; flash floods turn the M6 motorway into a waterway, and quietly murmuring becks become temperamental cascades of white spray. Perhaps too much is made of Cumbria's rainfall – the region has its share of long, hot summer days, although evaporation can cause morning mists that stifle the sounds of bleating sheep, and the mewing of peregrines on the crag tops.

Cumbria can boast of other superlatives apart from the weather: the highest mountain in England (Scafell); the deepest lake (Wastwater); the largest lake (Windermere); the highest lake (Broad Crag Tarn) and, as every Cumbrian knows, the smallest church (Wasdale) and the greatest liar – Will Ritson, the mid-nineteenth-century landlord of the Huntsman Inn, now the Wasdale Head Inn. which has just celebrated its centenary as the climbing centre of England. In the 1880's the fells and mountains provided a very challenging training ground for the Alpine mountaineering expeditions popular since the early eighteenth century. The cracks, flakes, slabs and buttresses of the Lakeland crags would be encountered in the big mountains only on a larger scale. Thus Scafell became a model for such as the Matterhorn and Mont Blanc, especially Scafell in winter – and this is why O.G. Jones climbed in January. John Stogdon, a Harrow schoolmaster and an enthusiastic Alpinist, wrote of Lakeland in 1870 ... 'not even in Switzerland do I remember any sight of mountains with more delicately beautiful outline, relieved against a clear winter sky.'

The Cumbrian mountains are a microcosm of Alpine scenery, but grouped together like an inverted bowl forming a rough circle about thirty miles across, the Lakes radiating from the centre. When in summer the evening light shimmers with atmospheric haze, the form, solidity and depth of the landscape is deceptive, the mountains recede towards the horizon in progressive shades of deeper blue and features may be hard to identify: is that Scafell Pike, or is it Great End, or Great Gable? The Durham-born writer Sid Chaplin knew of men 'who have gone year after year to walk the fells and crags and admit their inability to name the mountains'. As Hugh Walpole's Rogue Herries 'breasted the hill and turned back to look across Borrowdale the sky began to break. He stared, as though the scene was new to him:

never before had it held those shapes and colours nor would it again: with every snap of the shuttle it changed.'

A mountaineering handbook of 1893 described 'The little corner of England, known as the "Lake District" which is unsurpassed for its own peculiar form of beauty. It is comprised within a small area, and could be enclosed by a square having a side of twenty miles.' The book advised the visitor to 'rest content with tramps along the tops of hills; such walks can be devised in infinite variety, and will be found as full of interest as of beauty.'

Climbers come to the Lake District for the scenic beauty, for the historical associations with climbing and mountaineering, and for the seemingly endless composite *variations* that a crag can offer. The rocks were formed in Ordovician and Silurian times, some 400 million years ago, of shale, slate, limestone, sandstone and granite. Roughly speaking, the north is carboniferous limestone; the north-west is of Skiddaw Slate around Bassenthwaite Lake and north of Keswick and Derwentwater, Loweswater, Crummock Water and Buttermere. The main central area consists of igneous rocks of andesite and rhyolite and is known as the Borrowdale Volcanic series.

All the main climbing crags are formed of the Borrowdale Volcanic rock, ancient lava spewed out of volcanoes millions of years ago. The lava cooled and solidified, and later split and cracked under pressure. Denudation and weathering and the movements of glaciers also helped to create characteristic rock formations, the crags, outcrops, combes and valleys. The soil in some of the valleys is peaty, but on the fell sides and higher on the mountains the vegetation consists of bracken in profusion, hardy grass, club moss, hartstongue and maidenhair ferns, spiky bilberry plants, juniper, bell heather, heath rush and bog myrtle.

The sweeping mantles of scree flank the fell sides. When water freezes in cracks the expansion breaks up the friable rock, so screes are made up of stones that tumble down from the crags, varying in size from small rocks to large boulders. Gaps in the scree are swiftly invaded by heather, bracken and shrubs. Green lichen bestows some colour on the powdery-grey stones. In some places the scree is like a sloping roof of shale and green slate, but everywhere the solidity is deceptive: you can slip on the scree and slide for some distance on an avalanche of small stones or slate – indeed, the word 'scree' is derived from an old Norse word meaning 'to glide', as the word 'fell' comes from the Norse for 'rock.' The region has a long and romantic association with stones, if you accept the prehistoric and mysterious henges and stone circles, with their whispering of Druidic ceremony and ritual, as romantic. There are remains of more than thirty such circles in Cumbria, some among the largest in Britain: Carles at Castlerigg near Keswick; Long Meg and her Daughters; the Druid's Temple at Birkrigg. There were neolithic axe factories at Langdale and Borrowdale where axe heads were roughly hewn, and sent away to polishing centres at Shap, Portinscale and Clifton, where ancestral Cumbrians burnished the axes with sandstone.

Stone is everywhere. Stone cottages and farms, stone bridges, and the long marches of stonewalls that do not want of symmetry, and defy gravity on the steep-sided fells. The skill that shaped the axes is a legacy handed down to the stone wallers, and stone-knapping is the oldest craft in the world, thus Cumbrian men have a long and ancient relationship with the rock: the miners who dug through it to reach lead, iron ore and coal; the quarrymen who cut massive blocks of ornamental granite; the drywallers and shepherds who have walked the fells and climbed the heights of the crags for centuries, men with an inherent sense of balance and order, of solid inner strength and calm reserve, men of measured speech and re-strained gesture. Born climbers like Peascod and Jim Birkett, John Robinson and George Seatree.

The majority of Lakeland's greatest climbs, though, have been done by 'foreigners', by Lancashire lads such as Don Whillans and A.T. Hargreaves, and the Yorkshiremen F.W. Botterill, A.R. Dolphin, Allan Austin, Peter Livesey and Peter Whillance. So it is fitting that the first recorded Lakeland climb was made by a local shepherd. The shepherd was John Atkinson, and his objective was to climb to the summit of the remote Pillar Rock, 750 feet high, and located about five miles, as the buzzard flies, from Atkinson's home at Croftfoot, overlooking Ennerdale Water. Seen from Ennerdale, Pillar Rock stands proud and alone, dominating the landscape.

Atkinson chose a day in July, 1826, crossed the becks and ghylls of the Liza river valley, and climbed a thousand feet of grass, scree and rock to reach the base of the Pillar. He prudently chose an easy route, now known as the Old West route, while his collie dog waited below – according to accounts in the local press. The story takes on a certain old-world charm when compared to the description, by mountaineer Doug Scott, of Reinhold Messner's solo ascent of Everest in 1983 'while his girl-friend waited at the bottom.' Atkinson probably climbed Pillar because, like Everest, 'it was there' – a challenge to be taken up against the claim that the rock couldn't be climbed, though many had tried.

One wonders how Atkinson substantiated his claim to have reached the top. Did he take a friend as a witness, or invite the editor of *The Cumberland Paquet and Wares Whitehaven Advertiser* to record the event? The paper ran

That august body of gentlemen climbers (ladies were also admitted) the Fell and Rock Climbing Club of the English Lake District, in 1908. (F & RCC)

the story, describing in the best journalese of the period how Atkinson's dog 'uttered the most piteous cries during his absence.' In fact, the first personal account of a Lakeland climb, or rather descent, had been made some twenty years before by the poet Coleridge, who descended Scafell with 'limbs all of a tremble.' In 1864, the Rev. Julius Elliott, an early contender for the *Guinness Book of Records*, climbed Scafell, Great End, Great Gable, Kirkfell, Pillar Rock, Steeple, and Red Pike, all in eight and a half hours! Pillar Rock became the focus of Lakeland climbing, and by the 1870's several new routes to the summit had been established. 'Ascended Pillar Rock by Black Sail before breakfast', wrote one climber in 1877. Sixty years after the first ascent, tourists included a party of several ladies who, on reaching the summit, played cards to the accompaniment of guitar music. It was customary to place your visiting card in a bottle on the summit until two workmen on holiday pinched it. The rock was twice climbed by an octogenarian parson, the Rev. James 'Steeple' Jackson, who styled himself 'The Padre of the Pillarites', and who presumed it fair – on account of his venerable age – to employ a rope ladder, spikes and a hammer for the purpose, thus setting a precedent – ladders were used on several ascents thereafter. Two local climbers, John Robinson and George Seatree, were the first to use climbing rope in the Lake District, and Pillar Rock was the scene of the experiment, although Robinson confessed that he forgot the rope and left it on the top.

The technique of rock-climbing is essentially progressive – from the easy to the difficult to the impossible, although climbers will tell you that there's no such thing as an impossible climb. Every climb will one day be achieved, every mountain and hill made low. Once a climb has been made, others will repeat it, and thus a route is established, described and recorded in the guide books and magazines. Today, there are seventy-eight routes up Pillar Rock, of varying degrees of difficulty, and there is usually a climber or two on most days of the year scaling one of its many routes.

Since a rock represents a challenge to the climber, there's no point in merely repeating a climb over and over again. New routes or lines must be found, and new routes are progressively more difficult – that is their purpose. The development of climbing has been very well described by the Lakeland climber and geologist Frank Monkhouse as 'the interaction of three contributions: (1) the periodic appearance of an exceptional climber, ahead of his time, who pushed the standards of climbing well above the existing ones, thereby stimulating others to emulate and in due course surpass him; (2) the progressive improvements in technique and equipment; and (3) the discovery and exploration of 'new' crags, new, that is, in the sense that previously they had not been opened up because of their apparent inaccessibility, insignificance or vegetated appearance. The net result is that until the last few years (when progress has been very rapid, relentlessly so indeed) the story is one of periods when many new and evermore difficult routes are worked out, alternating with pauses for consolidation.'

Once a route has been viewed from below, the climber has to prove its viability – whether or not 'it will go.' Where the vertical line ceases, the climber will have to move horizontally to find another line of ascent, and thus executes a traverse. Many climbs are essays in speculation and empiricism, searching for handholds and the benign 'jugs' (holds like a jug handle or rung of a ladder – you should be so lucky ...!) that you hope are there – even a minute flake of quartz or silica will do if there is nothing else.

At a fundamental level, climbing is a physical manifestation of what psychologist Alfred Adler called 'the great upwards drive' of the psyche, the desire to reach the top, in climbing by the most difficult route, and the more arduous the climb, the more rewarding the achievement – *per ardua ad astra*. Added to this is the pleasure of the climb itself, the summit merely calling a halt to the exercise.

Once a new route has been 'put up' and established, it remains to name climb and grade it. Peter Whillance, one of the climbers featured in this book, said that by far the most difficult part of a climb was thinking of a name for it afterwards. The physical character of the rock gave the early climbs their names: Walker's Gully (named after a young climber who fell nearby); Hind Cove Gully; Central Slab Climb; Crack, Chimney and Slab; Grooved Wall. Many are eponymous, usually after the person who made the first ascent: Botterill's Slab; Haskett Buttress, Slingsby's Crack, Pendlebury Traverse. Apart from a few early examples, such as Sodom and Gomorrah on Pillar Rock, it was not until the late 1940s that the names of climbs began to stray towards the evocative and descriptive – Bill Peascod's Hailstorm, Cleopatra and Delilah – and later still in the 1960s we find climbs being called Megaton, The Dream Merchants, Paper Tiger, Apollo 8, and named after movies such as The Sting, The Blue Max and High Plains Drifter.

In 1897 the great pioneer O.G. Jones introduced a grading system based on the difficulty of the climb. These were Easy, Moderate, Difficult, Exceptionally Severe. Modern climbers still use the terms 'diffs and v-diffs' – but just *how* difficult depends on the climb and the climber. Later and more accurate grading systems appeared: Moderate, Difficult, Very Difficult, Severe and Very Severe. These gradings refer to the technical difficulty

'Feeling as small as a mouse climbing a milestone' Walter Parry Hasketh-Smith made the first ascent of Napes Needle on Great Gable in 1886. This feat marked the real beginning of rock climbing in the Lake District. (GPA)

Napes Needle in the 1890's, probably the most photographed rock in Britain, now well-worn through a thousand ascents. *Inset* The Needle in 1984, with climbers Dave Armstrong and Chris Bonington. (BT/GPA)

of making the moves to ascend, but perhaps more importantly the degrees of risk involved, and the risk of course increases with height, as we shall see.

O.G. Jones was one of a triumvirate of nineteenth-century climbers, each associated with a particular climb – Jones with Kern Knotts Crack, Walter Parry Haskett-Smith with the ascent of Napes Needle, and Frederick William Botterill with Botterill's Slab. All were men of considerable athletic prowess and courage, and in whom to a greater or lesser degree, the dull glint of fanaticism could be detected. Jones was a Londoner of Welsh descent; he was certainly eccentric, but perhaps it would be an exaggeration to say that he was mad.

A sepia photograph of Jones, taken by his fellow-climbers the Abraham brothers of Keswick, who were professional photographers, shows a man in his early twenties wearing a Norfolk jacket and soft, peaked cap. His expression is one of confidence, the eyes regard us levelly through gold-rimmed spectacles (he was short-sighted); under the slight moustache there is an even slighter smile. He wears a hemp rope over his right shoulder, hands rest on an ice-axe and he carries a rucksack. But a friend, William Crook, meeting Jones in the Alps, presents us with a quite different image: 'His face and hands were as brown as berries, covered with dust and sweat; his clothes were literally in rags, torn to pieces on the rocks.'

Jones, who reputedly dipped his fingers into boiling glue as a remedy for frostbite (his father was a carpenter), appeared indifferent to pain, fear or discomfort. He was lastingly enthusiastic, probably naïve although he secured an Honours degree in physics, and decidedly competitive. He was also very aware of the passage of time for he told Crook that 'there are only a few years in which I can do this sort of thing, and I want to get as much into them as possible.' He was a driven man, performing party pieces such as girdling a locomotive by using the rivets as handholds; climbing under and over a table without touching the floor, traversing a building on the outside wall, and the billiard room of the Wasdale Head Inn, hands on the billiard table and feet on the wall. How did he manage to stand still long enough for the Abraham brothers to photograph him?

Jones was a true 'tiger', as bold climbers became known, and pushed the frontiers of climbing forward with his ascent of Scafell Pinnacle from Lord's Rake in April 1898. Typically, Jones did the climb in his socks so that he could jam his toes into the zig-zag crack and execute a traverse with no hand holds. Jones's companion on the climb was G.T. Walker (also in his socks), though no relation to the youth who fell down Walker's Gully, and the climb had a particular significance in the evolution of the sport, by marking the transition from the 'gully and chimney' climbs to the far more challenging 'slab and wall' climbs, that is, scaling fully exposed the sheer face of the rock instead of the enclosed and less demanding chimneys. If you look back through history, the climbers first tackled the gulleys because these were the easiest courses. Then as time progressed they went up the chimneys – a gully is usually a wide watercourse, a chimney a wide crack – then they went for the corners, ribs, *arêtes* (ridges) and finer cracks. Climbers then progressed to the harder, more exposed areas of rock, the overhanging and bulbous faces, the walls and slabs. In so doing they increased the risk and the danger and thus served the true aims of the rock-climber: progressive difficulty. 'There are of course cliffs and crags that are all easy,' Pete Whillance explained recently. 'But inevitably there are crags with very hard potential routes that have to be left to the next generation. It may seem to the layman that a rock face is blank, yet it's very difficult to find a face that's *completely* blank. There are indentations, slight depressions, little pieces of quartz sticking out of the rock, that you can get some sort of purchase on. They *can* be climbed.'

Jones was the most flamboyant early-rising star of the sport, but the 'Father of British Rock Climbing' was Walter Parry Haskett-Smith, old Etonian and barrister, who in middle age looked more like Wyatt Earp than a respectable legal practitioner. When *in extremis*, Haskett-Smith was given to uttering epigrams from Homer in classic Greek. Descending the Pillar after an unsuccessful attempt at the summit, in 1890, Haskett-Smith slid his body over a block of stone wedged immediately above a precipitous slope. Just as he was about to drop down on the other side, he found that the massive stone was by no means firmly wedged and was coming over with him! 'My first idea was to pull frantically with my arms and force the mass back into equilibrium. It was like trying to straighten the Tower of Pisa. The rock came slowly over ... the pressure increasing frightfully with every minute of inclination.' It was then that he discovered that his waistcoat was entangled on the jagged edge of the rock. Hanging on with one hand he tore off his waistcoat and delivered the stone a vicious downward kick, which gave Haskett-Smith sufficient upward impetus, he writes, to clutch the hold above. The huge stone thundered down into the valley while he quoted Homeric verse. It might have been better, in the circumstances, had he managed to shout the warning *below!* in the manner of all climbers.

There were accidents, of course, and if experience was the best protection against death and injury, one can readily deduce that it was the inexperienced climber who was the most likely to 'come off'. This was indeed the

21

case on the Matterhorn in 1865 when Edward Whymper led a party of seven climbers to make a first ascent to the summit. The youngest and least experienced member of the party, Douglas Hadow, slipped and fell on top of the guide Michel Croz. The entire party were roped together, as was the custom of the time, and the combined weight of Hadow and Croz pulled off the Rev. Charles Hudson (a very experienced amateur) and then Lord Francis Douglas. Whymper and the remainder of the party would have gone too, had the rope between Douglas and Whymper not snapped as the four plunged to their deaths. It was, as Bill Peascod noted drily, 'the first *descent* of the Matterhorn'. Rope came into general use sometime during the mid-nineteenth century. A guide-book of the period stated that, 'The rule that a party should consist of not less than three on a rope is founded on the theory that if one slips or falls into a crevasse, two can hold him up and pull him out; whereas one probably could not.' The technique remained unquestioned for many years. Even thirty years later the lesson had not been learned, for in 1899 an almost identical tragedy occurred on the Dent Blanche. The party on this occasion consisted of F.W. Hill and O.G. Jones. They were accompanied by three guides, Elias Furrer, Jean Vuignier and Clemenz Zurbriggen. Furrer slipped, fell on Zurbriggen and Jones, and the three of them pulled off Vuignier. Hill's account was reported in the *Alpine Journal*: 'I turned to the wall to get a better hold, and did not see Vuignier pulled off, but heard him go, and knew that my turn would soon come. And when it did not I looked round, and saw my four companions sliding down the slope at a terrific rate, and thirty feet of rope swinging slowly down below me.' Jones's 'few years in which I can do this sort of thing' was sadly prophetic.

Techniques were subordinate to the fundamental aim of climbing the rock with style and élan. From the birth of climbing as a sport, climbing aids were generally thought to be unacceptable, especially the piton, a steel spike driven into the rock with a hammer – unless, of course, you had no alternative: 'There was only one thing for it,' M. Linnell reported of his struggles to surmount an overhang on Scafell, 'and it was an eventuality for which I had come prepared. I inserted a piton in the little crack, and inserted it well and truly with a hammer. Nor was it only put there as a safeguard; by pulling on it sideways, downwards, outwards, and upwards, and finally planting a foot on it, I was able, with a struggle, to reach a little ledge. I offer no apologies; those who prefer to climb the place unaided are cordially invited to remove the piton and do so.'

At heart, all climbers are purists, and prefer to eschew any kind of artifi-

Sunset over the north-western fells (AB)

cial aid between them and the rock. They are harsh in their judgements, warm in their praise and deeply reverent of true and original achievement, such as Haskett-Smith's ascent of the Napes Needle in 1886, by general consent the birth of British rock-climbing. The accolade awarded to Haskett-Smith for this feat was justified by the unique character of the rock, an isolated slim pillar that appeared to represent, for the pioneer Lakeland climbers, the very essence of endeavour and challenge, especially since the block that creates the pinnacle seems dangerously perched on its base. O.G. Jones thought the Needle 'a fine fellow as rocks go ... a gymnasium in itself.' When Haskett-Smith came along and decided to climb it, solo, and left his handkerchief on top as proof of his ascent, Jones declared that 'this first ascent is one of the most daring things that have been done in the Lake District.' One aspect of the Needle was ignored – its significance as a phallic symbol (Freud was as yet a young neurologist and the unconscious was still unconscious). It became a prime target to be conquered in an authoritarian age of stifling gentility. No wonder Haskett-Smith was dubbed 'The Father of British Rock Climbing!' There is a story, probably apocryphal as all the best stories are, that O.G. Jones was strolling down the Strand when he saw a photograph in a shop window. The picture was of Napes Needle, with figures perched on the top. The shot was a remarkable one for its time, and it had a considerable impact on Jones, whose interest in climbing was kindled from that moment. The picture had captured the attention of a number of passers by, several of whom vouchsafed the opinion that the climbers must be mad. 'Yes,' said Jones impatiently, 'but how did they get there?' 'That's easy,' came the reply, 'they've got a ladder round the back.' In fact ladders have been used from time to time – in 1954 a French team sneaked a seventy-foot ladder up the west face of the Dru on the second ascent to help scale awkward patches.

Only the professional class (including academics) and the rich had the leisure to climb. These were, in a literal sense, the social climbers, and the class barriers on the rock and in the mountains were only slowly eroded. Birkett, Peascod and Whillans were among the very few working class climbers to make any impact in the rock-climbing world.

As Bill Peascod explained, 'The centre of climbing was at Wasdale Head, the climbers went there at Easter and Christmas to get in practice for the big annual holiday in the Alps – that's what it was all about, training for the Alps. This circumstance existed right up to the turn of the century, but with somebody doing a climb for its own sake, every now and again, like the ascent of the Needle, and of Botterill's Slab in 1903.'

24

Botterill's Slab was not, as the uninitiated might suppose, a generous wedge cut from a farmhouse cake, but an important climb up the Central Buttress of Scafell. It was accomplished by Frederick Botterill, a slim, dark, bearded Yorkshireman who climbed in nail boots with his ice-axe between his teeth. Although climbing equipment was rudimentary, advances had been made. By Bill Peascod's time, in the 1930s, the basic gear was available.

In the 1890s, Jones, Solly and other climbers had introduced route inspection, where you were lowered from a 'top rope' (or you climbed up it) to reconnoitre the climb – a top rope was one secured from above. Routes were also cleaned of loose debris and grass, known as 'gardening.' ('Inspection' and 'gardening' were developed further in the 1920s by Kelly and in the 1970s by Livesey.) Veteran cragsmen and fell walkers now complain that the entire Lake District has been so thoroughly gardened by generations of climbers, that the crags look like steam-cleaned city blocks. By the mid-1920s the most significant advance was undoubtedly the running belay or 'runner' which allowed greater protection against falling, and so extended the limits of what was possible though it was still rare to have more than one running belay for each pitch.

Alpine hemp rope had already been introduced, and it was quickly adopted by climbers, but so was the potentially dangerous technique of roping together. Climbers usually worked together in pairs, the rope tied around their waists, although parties of three and four roped together were not uncommon – you can see this in the photographs taken by the Abraham brothers of Keswick, George and Ashley, who were fine climbers and mountaineers as well as being professional photographers. O.G. Jones, arriving in Keswick one morning in 1896, decided to call on the Abrahams, whom he had met briefly once at the Wasdale Head Inn. The trio quickly recognised their mutual passion for rock-climbing, and their meeting led to the sport becoming truly popular. Their important decision was to publish a book on the subject. Jones would be the author, it was decided, and the brothers would provide the photographs. Jones described the climbs and the locations, enlivened with gossip and anecdotes; the brothers photographed the rocks and posed, with Jones, in various climbing positions to illustrate technique. *Rock Climbing in the English Lake District* was published by the Abraham family in 1897, and was no mean effort to write, and photograph, considering the bulky equipment of the time. The three of them clambered up the scree hefting the big, brass-bound wooden whole plate cameras and sturdy tripods. They had the advantage, though, of dry photographic plates, and celluloid sheet film which had recently been introduced. They also used

25

wide-angle lenses which capture the broad expanse of the rock against which they would pose for the necessarily long exposures, while the other brother crouched under the black cloth. Once, Ashley Abraham emerged blinking from under the cloth, stepped backwards off a ledge, and was only saved by the fact that he was roped to his fifteen-stone brother George, who thus 'belayed' him against a fatal fall. Belaying to the rock was introduced by the Abraham brothers, and Jones was quick to see the advantages. On Scafell, he stood on Ashley's head to pass his rope through a bunch of stones jammed in a crack. George Abraham explained the technique thus: 'A careful watch should be kept for any small projections round which the rope can be slipped, and on extremely difficult places the leader may often thus secure safely. Moreover, in climbing difficult cracks small rocks are often wedged in the cleft and the rope can be threaded behind them. Standing on the smallest ledges, it is often possible to untie the rope end from the waist, thrust it up behind the stone, *from below*, be it noted, and then retie it on again.' The technique was not widely adopted, and the watchword was still 'one off – all off' so it was inevitable that a serious Alpine type of accident should occur in the Lake District. In 1903, four climbers, roped together, ascended the Scafell Pinnacle. They were all experienced, but it was a very blustery day and one of the team slipped, pulling off his four companions, or as Bill Peascod put it, 'all four climbers were spread out on the cliff, one came off and the whole four went down – plop, plop, plop, plop.'

To grasp the belaying principle, you have to imagine that you are climbing a cliff with a companion, and you are leading the way up. The rope is attached to your waist, and as you ascend your partner, or 'second', is standing on a ledge of rock below. He has secured the rope by winding it around a firmly rooted tree, or a natural spike of rock. The rope passes around his waist and around one forearm, and through the hands, to absorb friction in the event of a fall. He pays out the rope as you climb, until it is extended to, say, some twenty feet, at which point he stops, but if at twenty feet you cannot find a resting place or stance, your second continues to pay out the rope until you can halt. Then you belay your end of the rope while he climbs up and joins you. The span of rock-face between the two points of belay, or stance, the two stopping places, is called a 'pitch.' As climbing techniques progressed, and climbers become more confident, so the pitches lengthened, and longer run-outs of rope were employed.

Now, should you come off while climbing above your second, you will fall down to the belayed point where he is standing, and below him to a point where the rope stops your descent, unless, of course, the rope breaks.

It broke when Fred Botterill, a Yorkshireman and one of the great 'natural' and most graceful of climbers was doing a route to Eagle's Nest Ridge on Great Gable in 1909. His companion, Thomas Rennison, was leading while Botterill payed out the rope around a belay of rock. It is not clear from accounts just how far Rennison had climbed above his belay point, but it may have been as much as sixty feet. Rennison fell without a sound and Botterill, seeing him go, held tight to take the strain. The rope snapped at the belay point, possibly because the rope was too old and weak in places. Rennison was killed, and it is said that Botterill was so affected by the accident that he never climbed again.

'The belay made climbing that bit safer,' Peascod recalled, 'but although it was a vast step forward, it was a far, far cry from the refinements of today. The ropes we used were pretty much the same as they were at the turn of the century. We used the old manila hemp ropes, and we'd run out about 120 feet on a pitch without any belay in between, so you'd fall 240 feet and the rope would probably break. The longest run out I've ever done was 200 feet on a thin cord. I had nowhere to stop and had to keep going, which meant I was virtually climbing unprotected. With the advent of the belay, and later still the running belay, a new term entered the climber's vocabulary – the word 'protection', which simply means one's security against falling off. The great but short-lived climber (killed in the First World War) Siegfried Wedgwood Herford climbed the direct route to Hopkinson's Cairn on Scafell in one single pitch, trailing 130 feet of rope, and no belays. Like Jones he climbed virtually solo and in his socks. The degree of protection that a climb affords refers to the number of belayed points along a route, and the distance between them. If you climb with no protection at all, then you are virtually 'going solo.' In the climbing world, 'soloing' is a much used term, delivered with respect, cynicism or contempt, depending on the circumstances. To solo is to climb a route without any protection at all – no ropes, slings or chocks for belaying, just a bag of chalk to keep your fingers dry. Climbing with the conventional and accepted gear, ropes, slings and karabiners, is called 'free climbing'; climbing with points of aid, such as banging in pitons or using slings to stand in so that you gain height, is called 'artificial climbing'. There is a grey area between soloing and free climbing, where belaying points cannot be found and the climber is way up on the top of a long pitch with the rope paid out to 100 feet or more, so he has virtually no real protection, and this may be considered soloing. The climber didn't *mean* to solo – but that's how it turned out.

When Birkett and Peascod were climbing, protection gear was still minimal. Peascod climbed Eagle Crag in nailed boots, his only sling being used as a waist loop, attached to the climbing rope with 'an Army-surplus, D-link, screw gate karabiner – which I still have.' A karabiner, by the way, is a metal link with a spring-loaded gate, used for attaching to slings and ropes for belaying.

The breakthroughs that were achieved in pre-war climbing, and through the 1940s, were mainly psychological rather than technical, such as Jim Birkett's climb up Castle Rock, a route called Overhanging Bastion, and Bill Peascod's Eagle Front, the subject of our next chapter. Climbers stormed up routes by sheer determination, courage, and even their teeth, and Geoffrey Winthrop Young observed: 'A small but superlative class of climber already exists which specialises in unsound or uncertain holds. By a technique combining balance and a serpentine body-cling, the climber crawls adhesively up the face of vertical mud-verdure or of deciduous splinters unified by moss, not disdaining to use his teeth to maintain his balance, and his faith in the tenacity of Celtic turf to its native rock. The vegetarian technique has opened up for climbing, of a superselect order, a number of cliffs formerly shunned, or climbed only by their rotten gullies.' Banner Mendus, whose climb began this chapter, found 'places where a mouthful of heather was thankfully used as an additional support.' No, this was not 'aid' but a legitimate belay and emphasises the vigorous, resolute attitudes that were the foundation of the modern sport.

If rock-climbing was a means to an end – the end being Alpine ascents – it followed that climbs in the early days aimed for the summits of crags, fells and mountains. To climb a rock just for the sake of the exercise and technique was unknown until one day in 1893 when Jones, Robinson and W.H. Fowler, bored and restless, headed for the nearest rock mass they could find, and climbed Kern Knotts Chimney in the pouring rain. It was, so to speak, a 'rock-climber's climb', rather than a preparation for the mountains: a small scale attempt that was nonetheless challenging and difficult. During the climbs both Jones and Robinson had observed that the Kern Knotts Buttress sustained a long crack in addition to the chimney, and both had decided to tackle it in the future. Robinson defied Jones to climb the Kern Knotts crack but Jones eventually succeeded, first with a rope, then solo, and it became a classic climb by which later rock climbs were judged.

The pioneers climbed in their socks, and with their teeth, and persevered until their clothes were in rags. They hung on by the tips of their raw fingers and not infrequently fell to their deaths. Their dedication began an

evolutionary progress that required a rare courage, a single-minded determination, a unifying spirit, and a fine kind of madness. Some of those who
contributed to this progress, and are still contributing, are the subjects of
this book: Bill Peascod, the Cumbrian coal miner who climbed Eagle Front
in 1940; Don Whillans, the Salford plumber, who climbed Dovedale Groove
in 1953; Chris Bonington, the mountaineer, who nearly didn't climb the
challenging Holy Ghost route in 1965; Peter Livesey, the teacher who
changed the whole approach to climbing with his route Footless Crow, in
1974; Peter Whillance, appropriately a scaffolder whose fierce and almost
suicidal routes culminated in Incantations in 1984; and two of Britain's
finest women climbers, Jill Lawrence and Gill Price, both teachers, who
climbed Empire on Raven Crag in 1984.

Buttermere, with Crummock Water in the distance. Bill Peascod was the first climber to fully explore the north western fells. (AB)

Bill Peascod, an ex-miner and one of Cumbria's great pioneer rock-climbers. Peascod is now a successful landscape painter. (AB)

2

Bill Peascod: Eagle Front

It was fifty years ago that Bill Peascod – then a mere nine-stone strip of a lad – bicycled one magical summer morning from the colliery at Clifton, near Workington, to discover, for the first time, his Lakeland surroundings. In the 1930s Cumberland, like most of Britain, was still obstinately rooted in the mid-nineteenth century, and there were but two directions that a man could go: down the coal mines, or up in the fells with the sheep and the drywallers. Life was harsh on the fell farms but they had, at least, the wild beauty of the mountains, the noisy becks and gills, and the high tarns like 'a spoonful of blue in a cup of green hills', as H.V. Morton wrote of Rydal Water.

The coal miners knew nothing of this. Their horizons ended abruptly at the coalface from which, as Bill Peascod remembered, he and his father hacked ten tons of coal to fill twenty trucks every day. And if, like Bill Peascod, you were born in a mining town (Maryport, 1920) and in a mining family, as sure as coal is black you would go down the pit. English villages were tightly knit closed communities. Nobody travelled much beyond the parish bounds. In Bill Peascod's village there were no telephones, nobody owned a car, there was no electricity – only paraffin lamps and candles. 'The entire family life centred around mother and the hearth, the fireplace and the warmth, and reading. We used to spend a lot of time in winter nights doing hookie mats and prodded mats – these were great activities. They talk about real family life, but when I grew up in that village and went to work in the mines, there was a certain kind of grandness yet sadness about the life that young fellows led. Going out on Saturday and Sunday nights in your best blue serge suits and wearing lanky clogs.' Peascod smiles at the recollection. Fifty years ago might well have been two hundred years ago – so much has changed. 'Do you know what lanky clogs

32

were? Sharp pointed clogs, they were a bit prettier than the big clogs, they had wooden soles and leather uppers ... fronts with beautiful scroll patterns on them.'

The lads clonked down to the pub with the aim of getting plastered – you could get drunk, or near enough, on a few shillings a week. 'When the pubs closed the lads would return, chest flying wide open, red scarf hanging down, singing at the top of their voices – twenty or more in unison. But come five o'clock in the morning, on the first shift, dropping down the pit shafts in the cages, stinking of stale beer, everyone sorry for themselves. And then, at the bottom of the shaft, a three-mile walk to the working faces to fill ten tons of coal, and hope like hell you'd make enough money to go on the booze the following weekend – that's the way it went, along with the pigeon racing and dog racing and so on. I tried to keep out of it as long as I could, tried to look for something else, but in this part of the world there just wasn't anything else.' It was not only a routine of unremitting hard labour and discomfort but there was the ever-present sense of danger and fear. Mining accidents were commonplace, due to frequent breaches of safety regulations by the coalowners. Just three years before Peascod began work in the pits, the nearby colliery at Whitehaven suffered one of the worst disasters in the history of the area when twenty-seven men were killed in the Haig Pit. The disaster occurred as a result of shot-firing, which ignited the firedamp gas. In 1947, eighteen years later, the lesson still hadn't been learned and excessive shot-firing killed 104 miners in the same colliery.

The work was, in Peascod's words, 'desperately hard and nothing at all to do with mining of today – nothing at all. It was utterly depressing.' Bill Peascod laughs without humour as he says this, and shakes his head in mild disbelief as though it had happened to someone else. 'I went to work at the coal face when I was eighteen. We had to walk three miles to the coal face from the bottom of the shaft and you couldn't straighten up in many places. The seam itself was only twenty inches high. We worked at that all day, and when you'd filled your twenty tubs with coal, you turned round and walked back the three miles to the shaft. It was bloody hell upon earth.' It also influenced and shaped his character and his attitudes, to some extent, as it must have done to all those who worked down the pits. He has developed a deep tolerance and forebearance, and seems now at sixty-four to be a contented man though with an air of preoccupation. He escaped from what he undoubtedly saw as a life sentence in the pits by fierce determination and creative drive, and it began in an almost revelatory experience.

Bonington and Peascod heading for Birtness Crombe above Buttermere. Peascod was the first to explore the crags of the eastern fells. (AB)

Peascod with Bonington on Eagle Crag 1984, wearing socks over plimsolls, and using modern climbing gear. (PB)

'When I was eighteen I came out of the pit one morning, I'd been on night shift, and I cycled home from Clifton to Workington. It was one of the most beautiful English mornings that you get rarely, but when they come it's ... oh, wonderful! The light was shining over the fells and I could see the outline of the hills and everything was just incredibly beautiful. I got home and I had a bath – we didn't have any baths in those days in the pit, we used to go home and bath in front of the fire. My father had got in before me, and we had our plate of porridge, which is what we'd have for our meal coming off the pit. Then he went to bed, and I thought I'd go outside.'

In rural Cumberland you either walked, or you cycled, and people had no reason to go far beyond the bounds of their parish, except to go to work, or to market. But that morning, freed of 'all the stink and the sweat,' Bill Peascod succumbed to the spirit of adventure and discovery – and it was to change his life. 'I got on my bike and I cycled out – and I discovered the Lake District for the first time. I came to the top of Fangs Brow overlooking Loweswater, and although I lived no more than seven miles away from that place, I'd never seen it before, never even knew it existed. And I looked down at this beautiful morning, and I could hear the valley sounds, and everything was incredibly lovely, and my life and my destiny was shaped for me from that point.'

Peascod's destiny was to become one of Lakeland's great pioneer rock-climbers, and later in life a landscape painter of international repute. 'All my life I'd been conscious of the need to do something physical and I was interested in healthy outdoor activities. I'd glamourised myths like Tarzan of the Apes, where you could live a wonderful jungle life and grow big and strong – all this load of rubbish. So, whenever I could, I started walking out to the Lakes. I raided the local library and started reading everything that was ever written about Cumbria. I did long walks alone across the fells to Buttermere – thirty mile walks – and sometimes climb a mountain as well. Buttermere was my favourite valley – I think I had shares in it.' Had Peascod lived a century before, he might have met that other determined walker, a local boy (and no mean climber either) William Wordsworth, on 'One of those heavenly days that cannot die;

When, in the eagerness of boyish hope,
I left our cottage-threshold, sallying forth ...'

The fells seem to encourage solitude and introspection, and their scale is such that a man can walk in the high places with almost as much ease as down in the valleys, when keeping to the pathways and avoiding the scree. In the local library, Bill Peascod found Owen Glynne Jones's weighty book on rock-climbing, first published in 1897. 'I found then that climbing was my destiny, and I've climbed ever since – I was a natural, and there's no point in saying anything else, all good climbers are natural.' A would-be climber soon discovers whether or not he has the ability, the balance, the gift of surmounting the problems offered by a stretch of rock. Of course, among the 'naturals' there are bound to be those climbers who possess the gift to a marked degree – people like Peascod, Joe Brown, Don Whillans, Peter Livesey, and the other subjects of this book. Bill Peascod was helped, to some extent, by his trade. It was not just the psychological urge to break out of the black tomb and escape to the top of the crags which made Peascod a great climber, it was his physical fitness and development as well. In the 1930s, British miners were still using the pick and shovel and they were still using them in the late 1940s when European mines had all become mechanised. You wriggled your way through the pit props into the narrow seam and, supporting your shoulder on your shovel blade, you hacked the coal from the face with your pick. Then you slid off the shovel, and used it to throw the coal over your head on to the conveyor belt. It's fearsomely tiring, but it does give you well-developed arms and chest muscles. Also, because of the manner in which you hold the shovel, it gives you very strong fingers – perfect for hanging on to the rock.

There's a sort of quiet, controlled deliberation in Peascod's movements, a feeling of conserved energy. He has a good sense of humour, a generous warmth and an honest appraisal of his own abilities, and those of others. His first attempts at climbing were little more than scrambles up a steep incline, but here and there the routes went up steeper slabs of rock that required proper climbing techniques, using hand and foot holds and traversing ledges to gain ascent. Nevertheless, these were done 'solo' which means ascending without a rope. When you solo, you climb alone and without any protection against falling, although you can solo with a back-rope, a technique explained in a later chapter.

There are, as we shall see, many experienced climbers today who can scale a sheer wall of rock, many hundreds of feet high, with the ease of a gecko climbing a mission wall, and without any equipment save a pair of rubber-soled climbing shoes and a bag of french chalk to absorb the perspiration on the fingertips. The climbers of Peascod's generation however never dreamed of this sort of approach to climbing. 'My first climbs were solo, then I thought I'd better have a rope. All the best climbers in the

Eagle Front is the classic climb of Buttermere: very severe and with eight pitches, it was first climbed by Peascod in June, 1940. (PB)

Bill Peascod. Leading first ascent of Resurrection, High Crag. (1944) The climb was done in nailed boots and rain. (BP)

Bonington and Peascod on top of Eagle Crag, Birtness Crombe, after their climb for the television camera. During the climb Peascod was obliged to stand on Bonington's head for five minutes while he searched for a hold, 'the old traditional combined tactics way'. (BT)

39

photographs had ropes and big nailed boots, so I nailed myself a pair of boots, and bought a fifty-foot length of very thin manila hemp, and tied it around my waist, and dragged it up the climb behind me, hoping it would stick on to something if I fell off. . . .'

For a time, Peascod kept his climbing activities more or less to himself, since the majority of people in the Lakes in those days thought climbers daft – and there are not a few, even today, who still think so. Peascod decided, though, that he had to tell his father. 'He never raised any objections,' Peascod remembers, 'nor indicated concern or pride.' The taciturn insularity of the daleman does not allow emotion to be easily expressed. 'Yet I've discovered since that he had a great deal of concern and pride for me.'

When Bill Peascod took up climbing, techniques and equipment were still fairly primitive, and owed more to the lessons learned in the Alps than on British rock. The rope, as Peascod explained, came in as an aid in the last century. 'In theory it was supposed to secure climbers together, but its main function really was to secure everybody but the leader. The leader in those days, more often than not, was a highly experienced Swiss peasant who called himself a guide, and they eventually became full-time professionals – they never fell off, they couldn't fall off, they *daren't* fall off!'

Now, this is something that you'll often hear from veteran climbers, and it puzzles the novice. After all, 'not falling off' seems to imply, in some way, that you are in control of your fate. But the experienced climber *is* in control, by knowing just how far he dare go. The rock-climber and mountaineer Don Whillans, now aged fifty and weighing fourteen stone owing to his partiality for draught ale, sees falling off (or 'coming off' as climbers prefer to say, as if they did it voluntarily) as the result of bad miscalculation. 'When I was climbing hard that was summat you never did, and that's why I don't think I ever climbed to my absolute limit because, at the back of my mind, I knew I mustn't fall off. I've spent too many bloody years knowing that if I fell off it would be a serious do. I'd either be badly injured or killed, and it would be due to bad calculation, and the climb is more difficult than I had anticipated.'

Today, apparently, falling off is an intrinsic feature of climbing – all the best people do it. 'The present day approach to climbing,' said Peascod, 'is that you are bound, sometime or other, to take a fall. Pre-1950 the thought of falling off was, well, you just didn't do it. I like to say that what we did in those days was to erect some kind of 'performance barrier' – a limit both physical and psychological, and you'd climb up to that barrier. Obviously it wasn't your ultimate limit. Your ultimate limit was when you fell off, but you climbed some way towards it and suddenly a little thing inside your head would say, 'Look, mate, back off now as you're getting near.' So you developed an ability to assess just how far you could take chances. You could still reach a very high standard of climbing, and you were still prepared to do things knowing that it was within your ability.'

Had Bill Peascod and his generation been in possession of modern equipment – the machined metal wedges, nylon ropes, tape slings, bags of chalk – which we will come across in later chapters – they certainly would have improved their standards of climbing, but even so they would have lacked the attitude and approach of today's hard-nosed, competitive 'activists'. In Peascod's day, climbing was the sport of gentlemen and players, but 'with the gentlemen outnumbering the players by a thousand to one.' Also many more inexperienced climbers were scrambling up the crags, while today fledgling climbers take wing quite rapidly, due to the technical literature available, and the climbing walls in sports centres, where one can train in the evenings.

'In the old days, I'm talking now about pre-1940, there was probably a greater percentage of fatal accidents among the climbing fraternity than there is now, largely among those with little experience. The majority were killed falling down easy gullys on their way back from a climb. This was usually because they were switched off, they'd overcome the difficult bit and had relaxed. They were not paying attention.' Descent from a summit can release feelings of euphoria, elation, a sense of anti-climax, and carelessness.

According to the moral ethics of the day, being killed was acceptable, but being competitive was not, at least, not overtly so; rock-climbing and mountaineering tested one's mettle and one's endurance according to the fairly strict rules of the game. That is why climbing clubs were formed, and rules laid down as to the use of aids for climbing; ropes were necessary but pitons were frowned upon – and anyway, they were foreign.

Since wherever Englishmen form a common interest they will found a club, it was a matter of a short time before climbing clubs began to appear. That august body, the Alpine Club, was already a voice of authority in mid-Victorian times, but the turn of the century saw the foundation of several Scottish Clubs, the Ladies' Alpine Club, and in 1907 the Fell and Rock Climbing Club of the English Lake District, which elected Ashley Abraham as the first President, and John Robinson and George Seatree as Vice-Presidents. One of the members was L.J. Oppenheimer, killed in 1916, whose exploration of the Buttermere fells even predated Peascod's pioneer climbs.

When Bill Peascod bought himself a hemp rope, in the 1930s, rock-climbing had attracted considerable numbers from among the professional classes, from the undergraduates who used their new expertise to scale the perpendicular heights of King's College chapel at night as a prank: '... the ground is precisely one hundred feet directly below you. If you slip, you will still have three seconds to live.' The art of stegophily (building-climbing) resulted in Winthrop Young's *Guide to Trinity Roofs*. In those days one climbed with restraint and due modesty. One of the foremost rock climbers before the Second World War, Dr J.M. Edwards, recorded an occasion where he climbed up to fifteen feet and, though the route stretched up ahead of him, failed to gain an inch. He reached into his pocket, pulled out a tin of sardines, and ate the contents, then he climbed down and headed for home.

The main area for Lakeland climbing was still centred on Wasdale, Great Langdale, with Borrowdale lagging behind and Buttermere relatively unexplored. Then in 1939, as the Fell and Rock Climbing Club recorded, 'Bill Peascod appeared on the scene ... raising the standard of climbing in the area by a full grade, with his Far East Buttress route in 1940. A year later he boldly girdled Eagle Crag, appreciated the feasibility of a way up the main face and returned a fortnight later to complete what remains the classic route of the area, Eagle Front.'

By 1939, Bill Peascod had been climbing alone for two years, because he couldn't find anyone else to climb with him, and he chose Buttermere and the north-western fells because they were his home ground. 'I never knew any person who either walked the hills or climbed rocks who came from the same background as mine. Eventually I got to know a fellow called Jim Birkett, a miner and quarryman from the iron-ore mines in Millom. So I would say, without much fear of contradiction, that as far as the Lakes are concerned, Jim Birkett and myself where the first of the working-class element to make any significant contribution to climbing.' Then Peascod joined one of the climbing clubs and discovered a member who lived in the same town. This was S.B. Beck. 'He was the very first person I ever climbed with, and the standard just rocketed up from then on, because he was a very fine second, just the sort of catalyst that I needed to get me up the crags. In fact, it was with Bert Beck that I did Eagle Front, and some of the best climbs for which I'm known.'

Novice climbers to the Lakes soon discover that the crag they are aiming to climb is often a considerable distance from any road or habitation. Not only do you have to climb the crag, but you have actually got to walk there first; only film crews have the benefit of helicopters. More often than not, the crag is an hour's or even a two hour's slog up a steadily ascending path, around boulders and over swollen streams. The way will be boggy in places, in others crisp and scratchy with bilberry and bell heather. Eagle Front is Bill Peascod's pioneer route up Eagle Crag at the head of Birkness Coombe. The crag is a magnificent wedge-shaped buttress which dominates the upper coombe, reaching a maximum height of 500 feet, but it gets little sun and has a forbidding atmosphere. The approach to the Coombe is from Gatesgarth Farm, a walk of over an hour, up the side of a gurgling beck and over the drystone walls where you may see 'the Herdwick sheep pouring through narrow gullets of stone as the beck flows through the gills.'

Given the average Lakeland weather where the fine rain slants horizontally across the fells, the north-facing Eagle crag is more likely to be wet and greasy than dry, and in the wet a climb can be of epic proportions. 'Epic' is a term that climbers use to describe a climb with unforeseen problems. For example, and just to diverge momentarily from the main route, Chris Bonington recalled an epic 'when Doug Scott and I climbed the Ogre in the Himalayas, and Doug fell off the top while abseiling and broke both legs, and we had a hell of an epic getting back down again. We ran out of food, I then fell off and broke my ribs and got pneumonia, and I was very ill and weak and it went on for a long time.' *That's* an epic. Anyway, there are many routes on Eagle Crag, and some of them are extremely severe, such as The Plague Dogs and Deimos, but Eagle Front remains the classic, following a devious but logical route up the main face.

'It's a big climb,' explains Peascod, 'but not in terms of difficulty by today's standards, but on that second pitch, which is 90 feet long I had no runners at all. When I did Eagle Front I did it stone cold. I'd never been on that part of the crag before, I didn't do any prior inspection, just followed my nose up it. Usually, any inspection was done from below, or a climb nearby, or from across the valley. You can see the line that you'll follow, and the holds and the cracks. The trouble with Eagle Front is that they looked like big holds but when you got there they all sloped the wrong way. When we climbed in the area it was virtually virgin territory. We were there first and we'd got more to choose from. In 1940 you could count on one hand the number of people who were leading climbs of a high standard in the Lake District; the majority of our climbs were done in Buttermere, the remainder in Newlands and in Borrowdale.'

On Eagle Crag and neighbouring Grey Crag, Peascod pioneered no less than fifteen major routes, and Eagle Front was the first Very Severe climb he and Beck had ever attempted. As it felt harder than anything that they had so far done, they tentatively labelled it VS. The climb has practically everything – ribs and grooves and slabs and cracks and a long traverse. There are eight pitches, one of 95 feet which offered no protection to Peascod when he first climbed it, 'but the main difficulties are over in the first sixty feet of the pitch. When I did it I was only twenty, young and daft, with great bloody confidence – until about a month later when I picked up my first dead body at the foot of Pillar Rock, and that slowed me down a bit. Slowed the lot of us down. A young lad of eighteen, he'd been soloing and fell off the nose, 300 feet. This very strange thing happened – we were going across the back of the Rock, and I heard a curious sound, like a pigeon flying off a roof. Wings flapping. We didn't associate it with anything until later in the day when we found the body. It must have been his clothes rattling as he hurtled downwards . . .'

On Eagle Front, and other climbs of the period, Peascod carried a hemp rope and a pair of Woolworth plimsolls. The ropes in the wet became like wire hawsers and were as difficult to bend as a horseshoe. As for the plimsolls, you bought them a size smaller than your usual foot size and then hacked off all the rubber around the edges – they crippled your feet, but it meant you could force your toes into tight spaces. Sometimes even that was insufficient, and Peascod would remove his plimsolls and climb in his socks – one shoe in his mouth, the other down his shirt front. They had become 'okay' footwear since Harry Moss Kelly had introduced them in the early 1920s. In those days climbers wore nailed boots, and the climbing world probably thought Kelly an absolute rotter for wearing plimsolls – until they began to hear about his climbs. Kelly predated Peter Livesey's approach by inspecting from a top rope, preparing for belays and gardening – all rather unorthodox, but effective. In 1926 Kelly did the magnificent Moss Ghyll Grooves on the Central Buttress of Scafell, which he had had in mind for seven years. His contribution to Lakeland rock climbing, apart from the plimsolls, was his clinical technique and his emphasis on the importance of *descending* from climbs (first suggested by Herford) as a means of improving technique. For Kelly 'there was no place like Wasdale Head. I lost my heart to it, so that when Morley Wood tried to inveigle me to Wales by talking about a 'mighty unclimbed cliff' called Clogwyn du'r Arddu, I am afraid] turned a deaf ear to his entreaties.'

Kelly was climbing a good fourteen years before Bill Peascod began hi series of thirty pioneer routes in Buttermere, and Peascod still used naile boots on some of his climbs or wore his socks over his plimsolls, never pre-inspected his routes, nor did he garden. This was partly due to the slow acceptance of new methods, but largely, in Peascod's case, because he hadn't the time – Bill Peascod was a Sunday climber, even in the rain. Eagle Front was first climbed on a Sunday, when Peascod could reach for the sky instead of plunging down the pit shaft to 'the bloody hell upon earth.'

He dreamed of escape from the mines, and frequently discussed it with Bert Beck, who made a suggestion that few miners would have thought of. 'You'll never get out of the pits during the war,' said Beck (because coal mining was vital to the war effort) 'so you might as well make a study of it. Go to evening classes.' Peascod studied at the local technical college and later qualified as a mining engineer, becoming an under-manager in the colliery at the age of twenty-five. Escape from the coal face had whetted Peascod's appetite for higher things – not just the crag tops, but a balance of the cerebral against the physical. 'I'd always been academically inclined, even though I had had a poor basic education. The management job didn't fulfil my needs, it gave me a good income, but there was too much conflict between my climbing and the industry.' At some point in their lives, all serious climbers find that the sport, or the pastime, is in conflict with their profession and their work. Whillans, Bonington, Livesey, Whillance all decided to become professional or semi-professional, often with the prim disapproval of the conservative climbing fraternity; Bonington's fund-raising activities in support of his Everest Expedition in 1975 was seen as publicity-seeking self-interest, but Peascod is full of genuine admiration. 'It's only because he's successful, he's made it work. You see, Chris said to me once, 'People ask me what I do for a living, and I tell them I'm a climber.' Other people may say, I'm a bookseller, or a teacher – but he's a climber! He's made it! He's done what so many of us would like – well, I'd have given my right bollock to have done that in 1950.'

Once he had qualified, Peascod taught at the local college, and was at the top of the teacher's pay scale in 1952. He had also put up over fifty major routes since Eagle Front, culminating in the two VS routes, Eve and Delilah. It was then that Bill Peascod decided to emigrate, and for the most simple reason in the world – 'I needed the money. I couldn't afford a car, I didn't drink, I didn't smoke, I could not afford holidays. In the end, Australia was very good to me and gave me a lot of opportunities that I would never have got in Britain. When I went there to teach I had only twelve students, but when I left I was in charge of mining studies in four colleges, and in numerous outlying centres.' Peascod lived in Australia for twenty-seven years, 'and I missed England every single day. The loss of the Lake District and climbing was intense. For years and years I dreamt every night of coming back, and I was bitterly homesick. I tried all sorts of things, like studying mathematics for three years. I took up painting to try and fill the void, and painted Australian landscapes. I couldn't paint babies and nudes and flowers – but do you know what my wife said, recently?' Peascod is married to a young and pretty Japanese girl, and they live in a farmhouse at the foot of Skiddaw. 'She said, those Australian landscapes were not of Australia, they were here – you were painting the Lake District.' 'Twenty seven years I was in Australia, yet it's as if it never happened at all – a period in my life that I have totally blanked out. I don't think I ever left here, really.'

When Bill Peascod returned from Australia he was sixty. One of the first things he did on his return was to re-climb his old routes, including Eagle Front. But now he had the modern gear, the nylon ropes and slings, metal chocks and chalk. 'We are very much into the modern idiom of cleaning it all from the top, with a wire brush.' Peascod says this with a straight face and no hint of cynicism. 'With the modern equipment I find I can get up climbs as hard as ever before, but it would be ludicrous to imagine that I'm climbing as well as I could at, say, thirty-two, when I was at my peak.' There is no evidence of the intolerance associated with an older generation for the impatient, pushy newcomers and their abrasive competitiveness. 'I don't find them abrasive. They are abrasive to each other, but not to me – I'm an antiquarian and no challenge whatever. They look at me with a sort of filial interest and say – to themselves – 'You silly old bugger' – but I get on with a lot of the lads very well, and they confide in me, but were I intent on grabbing a route from their fingertips. ... I know perfectly well that in order to get up these hard routes they have to be in constant training, and watch their weight and calorie intake. Every new generation that comes along looks at a climb and says – that face, that crag, is impossible! The next generation will come along and climb it. It's like breaking the mile record – there's no ultimate, until they run out of crag space.'

Bill Peascod, ex-miner, mining engineer, lecturer, pioneer rock-climber, is now a full-time painter. The drive, the need to be involved with an obsession, is still there. If there is a hint of sadness, it may be on account of the wasted years away from the Lakes. I asked him when he last climbed.

'A rock? Yesterday. I still do quite a bit. My best year since I came back was in 1982 when I climbed seventy-seven days, I kept a notebook.'

Any new routes?

'Yes, I did one the day before yesterday – it wasn't very hard, but I did one.' At an age when many climbers of his generation, and even the generation following, nod off in front of the clubroom fire, Peascod is still putting up new routes. He came close to an acceptable definition of the climber's philosophy when, at the base of Eagle Crag, one typical summer day in the driving rain, he and Chris Bonington discussed the purpose of propelling themselves up sheer rock faces.

'I climb,' said Peascod, 'because I was good at it. I was an absolute natural, as I said before, and if nothing else was natural to me, *that* was. Also, it's the adrenalin and the bloody ego, there's no doubt about it, knowing that you've pioneered a difficult climb and not many other people have. It satisfies a primitive need. There's something tremendously exhilarating inching up a steep slab and reaching your hand up and there, at last, is a magnificent hand hold, and you curl your fingers round it, and all your birthdays come at once.' Peascod chuckled, wiping the raindrops from his glasses. 'And suppose it isn't there? Then you're in trouble, and you just have to go on 'till you find one.'

3

Don Whillans: Dovedale Groove

At first sight, Don Whillans would fit perfectly in a French village. He wears, indoors and outdoors and probably in bed, a corduroy cap, or a flat peaked cap of Prince of Wales check with a button in the centre. A white vest shows in the V-neck of his big pullover, worn with khaki drill trousers and plimsolls. Whillans is broad, stocky and muscular and admits to weighing around fourteen stone. A grizzled, grey beard and weathered complexion suggest just now and again, especially when he narrows his eyes, a man it would be unwise to cross. Give him a glass of wine and a packet of Gauloises and he would resemble Jean Gabin, except that when he opens his mouth, he delivers pithy comments with a gruff, Salford accent. And he wouldn't thank you for the wine – he can't bear the stuff. What Don Whillans most enjoys is a jar of ale with the lads. His friends down the pub might include Joe Brown, with whom he has been most closely associated, Mo Anthoine, or Pete Whillance ('E's good for a jar, is Pete'), and Bill Peascod, who sometimes comes to visit Whillans in Penmaenmawr, North Wales. He and Peascod then climb together, two great veterans tackling slightly less taxing routes than when in their prime. Of Peascod, Whillans said, arched eyebrows under the cap, 'I'm amazed at him, you know. He come here, the other week, and bloody 'ell, he was itching to get on to the rock and that, but it wasn't that good and everything was very wet, and me – I only want to climb if it's reasonable.' Peascod laughs. 'He's a good lad, is Don, I get on very well with him.'

So do most people, in spite of his reputation for being 'hard and uncompromising – the ultimate toughie.' Whillans' lack of height – he is 5 foot 3 inches – was ('was' because he seems to have mellowed somewhat) well compensated for by his pugnacity, and his ability to meet trouble halfway. 'He stood out,' said Joe Brown, 'as more aggressive than anyone I've met

48

before, or since. He wasn't frightened of anyone or anything, and he had a reputation for fighting, for "having a go". But he's the man to be with in a tight corner.' In the mountains Whillans had a shrewdness and a sixth sense that has more than once saved him and his companions from injury and death. He has become one of Britain's greatest mountaineers. Whillans has given everything he has got to climbing. With a dogged tenacity, and dedication that is almost old-fashioned, compared with today's studied and competitive approach, he can be both 'a toughie' and a big softie. 'He's sincere and honest, and generous to a fault,' said Nat Allen, an old friend and climbing companion,' but he doesn't wrap anything up, he just tells you exactly what he thinks.' The climbing world has great respect for Whillans, and it wouldn't stretch a climbing rope too far to say that many love him as a sort of ideal folk-hero and one who reflects the climbing fraternity's own views on most issues. But perhaps this is now true only of his own generation, and the generation that followed. Of the new wave of athletic climbers who train hard, diet and drink orange juice, Whillans has mild contempt. 'Oh, aye, they climb better but they're a pain in the arse.'

Whillans is now fifty-one, but his most famous climbs, put up in the 1950s, were renowned for their directness and challenging difficulty; they simply went straight up and over the top. His attitude to climbing was recalled by Chris Bonington, who teamed up with him in 1961. 'We spent the whole of that summer mostly just sitting below the North Wall of the Eiger, waiting for it to come into condition for climbing, but it never did, and Whillans wasn't prepared to go snow-climbing. "I'll only do a climb if I'm really interested in it. It's got to be a good line – not just hard – but one that catches my imagination."' Instead of climbing the Eiger, Whillans and Bonington pioneered a new route up the Central Pillar of Freney on Mont Blanc, with the late Ian Clough, and Jan Djuglosz. Bonington then wrote of Whillans: 'This summed up his entire attitude to climbing – all the routes he had put up in England and Scotland had been superbly direct, uncompromising lines – ones that hit you in the eye as obvious, but at the same time were too difficult, or more often too frightening, to have been done by anyone else. To this day, some of his climbs rank among the most formidable in Britain.'

Donald Desbrow Whillans was born in Salford in 1933 and like Bill Peascod he left school at fourteen to start work. His father was a grocer. Whillans and his partner Joe Brown were the first lads from the working class who broad-shouldered their way into the middle-class climbing world, the world of academics and professional men. As far as Whillans was con-

Don Whillans, one of the founder members of the famous Rock and Ice Club, a bunch of hard, imaginative climbers who set up new records in the early 1950's. Whillans later became one of Britain's leading mountaineers. (AB)

Dove Crag, Dovedale, 'one of the steepest cliffs in England,' where Whillans, Brown and Cowan put up Dovedale Groove in 1953. (BT)

Whillans, the mountaineer, giving the thumbs-up on the first ascent of the Central Tower of Paine in Patagonia, which he climbed with Bonington in 1962. (CB)

cerned 'gentlemen' climbers had nothing at all to do with climbing. 'I heard about the 'old school tie' and frankly I didn't know what they were talking about. People used to start climbing as I did, by first walking in the mountains, then you'd do easy rock-climbs, then you'd find out that you were a better climber than you thought, so you'd get on to the harder climbs. If that's the orthodox way of doing it, that's how I started.' There was also a certain amount of parental encouragement: 'My father was a very keen rambler, and he used to take us kids out into Derbyshire, Edale and all those places. I used to go by myself some weekends walking thirty miles a day and one Sunday I met this Eric, a fellow who was in my class at school, he was out walking too. I got chatting to him and said, "Fancy coming over the tops?" and he said, "Aye, why not?" So we began climbing together at weekends.' Their first climb was called Atherton Brothers on Shining Clough, a gritstone outcrop. It was rated Severe, but Whillans had no knowledge of grades, he simply soloed it. 'Thank Christ for that,' he gasped when he got to the top. 'It was the first climb I did, and I never did another quite like it. Then I bought a rope.

'I thought climbing rope should be thick enough to get hold of, so I went to a ship's chandler in Manchester. It was completely the wrong length and weight, and we hadn't been climbing with it very long when we met some proper climbers who advised us to buy thinner ropes of Italian hemp.' The two friends began climbing on the gritstone edges of the Peak District. They learned about snaplinks, slings and karabiners, and were able to give themselves some protection and tackle more strenuous climbs. Then Whillans heard stories about a plumber called Joe Brown, and Joe Brown heard about a plumber's apprentice called Whillans, although Brown had the edge over Whillans, in terms of climbing experience, by about five years. By a remarkable coincidence they were both climbing in the same district and more or less at the same standard. They were to become the most famous double-act in modern climbing history, and a hard one to follow by virtue of the difficult routes they put up together.

Nat Allen remembers Whillans as 'an ordinary, quiet little lad of about sixteen or seventeen, although always a strong character,' and says that the Whillans-Brown partnership was formed on a gritstone route called Valkyrie Direct on the Roaches in Staffordshire. Allen recalls that Whillans 'simply floated up it. From the start he was a fantastic performer, and incredibly gymastic.'

Brown and Whillans were both small, both fit, and 'like peas in a pod. A team, and not competitive against each other.' Their climbing styles were

Whillans on Dove Crag, Dovedale, 1984, over thirty years since he and Joe Brown pioneered their classic route Dovedale Groove. (BT)

Don Whillans, left, with Chris Bonington at Brotherswater in 1984, with the plimsolls, nylon rope and karabiners of the 1950s. (AB)

Riding pillion with Whillans, said Chris Bonington, was 'a hell of a lot more frightening than most of the climbs I've done'. Setting off for the Eiger in 1962 and in 1984. (BT/DE)

quite different, and complementary. Brown went up the crags sloth-like, 'with not much air between him and the rock' as Allen put it. Whillans, by contrast, was agile as a monkey. 'Don swings off, flies into space, hardly seeming to touch the rock.'

Breaking the commandment 'thou shalt not fall off', Whillans frequently did fall in the early days. Belayed by his second, Ray Greenall, he fell more than forty feet from a route called Peapod, bouncing off the rock during his descent, while the rope sang through Greenall's hands, skinning his palms and causing burn marks to his arms. Whillans hurled himself into the air and touched down at the bottom of the cliff, almost unscathed.

At nineteen, Whillans was earning £3 a week working for a firm of central heating engineers. In the evenings he went to night school to learn to be a plumber, and after night school he would go on to the Levenshulme Palais to meet his friends and decide what they were going to do at the weekend. They talked about climbing – what else? They did not have much money, but one of them, Don Cowan, did have a motorbike. On Saturday mornings Whillans had to work, 'and I didn't get paid until Saturday dinner, so I couldn't leave without me wages.' They all met at the bus garage in Mersey Square, Stockport, and on Saturday afternoons would take the bus to Froggatt Edge in Yorkshire, or the gritstone edges that surround Manchester. Looking back, Whillans says, 'It wasn't an awful lot of fun, really – I can't even remember if there was television or not, in those days.' If he couldn't go by bus, he hitch-hiked. Don Whillans was perforce a Sunday climber – while Don Cowan and Joe Brown went to the climbs by motorbike, Whillans went by bus. 'I used to get one day's climbing a weekend while they got two, and several of the new routes were done on Saturdays so I missed out.'

One of the new Whillans/Brown routes was put up on Cenotaph Corner on Dinas Cromlech in Snowdonia, and Whillans' account of it clearly reveals his determination. 'Inch by inch, I got to the crux move where the holds on the wall seemed to disappear. I saw one which was a sort of pocket ... so I reached up and grabbed it. It turned out to be full of razor-sharp little flakes which cut my fingers pretty badly but I knew it was the key. After a time I launched up and made my move and that was that. We knew we had virtually cracked it because Joe had seen the last pitch from the Corner and he knew it would go. We called it Cemetery Gates after a bus we saw in Chester.' Eventually, Whillans was able to buy a bike. 'Me first bike was a Royal Enfield 350 and it cost £120, but me dad lent me the money, and it took me about three years to pay him back.' After climbing came motorbikes – and they are still the main preoccupations in Whillans life. He currently owns three bikes, one of them a monster almost as big as himself and with whom he has much in common, they both operate best at full throttle; Whillans has had more accidents while motorcycling than while climbing.

The group of young enthusiasts met every weekend and they tackled the hardest climbs they could find; they were the working-class tigers, and their like had never been seen before in the climbing world. They were the new elite. Whillans recalls that someone suggested forming a club. 'Nobody was very enthusiastic at the time, it didn't really seem necessary, but you'll always get some bugger that wants to organise things. Joe had this book by Andre Roche called *Rock and Ice* and that's how we got the name of the club, like.' The Rock and Ice Club was to become as famous as its founders. It was formed in 1951, and of the club Allen Austin wrote: '. . . the new group of tigers from Wales, the "little men" of the Rock and Ice. In other districts these men proved to be the most formidable group of climbers ever to operate on British rock. In Langdale their offerings were less important than elsewhere – but notable for all that.'

Brown and Whillans consolidated their partnership and began tackling some of the North Wales climbs, in particular Dinas Cromlech on which they put up Cemetery Gate, Cenotaph Corner, and the Girdle Traverse, while on Cloggy (Clogwyn d'ur Arddu) they did Vember, Taurus and Black Cleft. 'Joe and I were climbing a pretty similar standard then, fairly equal. Since those days I've put on a lot of weight but Joe – I call him "The Incredible Shrinking Man", he seems to get lighter. He's shrivelling up! He, he!' Whillans chuckles hoarsely. In 1953, when Whillans was twenty, he and Brown sought out new routes in the Lake District. It was a brief hiatus in pioneer climbing. Bill Peascod, champion of the Buttermere fells, emigrated to Australia; the prolific Lakeland climber Arthur Rhodes Dolphin was killed on the Dent du Geant in the Alps in 1956, and the laurels were awaiting Allan Austin. Then Whillans, Brown, Nat Allen and Don Cowan arrived on their bikes and put up Triermain Eliminate on Castle Rock.

Two months later they explored the possibilities of Dove Crag, limbering up on the existing route called Hangover, which Nat Allen led. Then came Dovedale Groove. There was no pre-inspection, abseiling down from a top rope or anything. They just went straight up it, Whillans leading and gardening for Brown and Cowan who had to dodge the turf as it came flying down. The climb requires strenuous bridging (straddling with the feet either side of the groove, a groove being – roughly speaking – the V-shape formed

by the meeting of two walls) and jamming with hands and arms. The route takes in an overhanging groove and overhanging crack, with four pitches.

The Rock and Ice Club now extended the existing grades to include Extremely Severe, and Exceptionally Severe. 'The difference between the two', said Chris Bonington, was that the former was a route of great seriousness and length, while the latter was of great technical difficulty, but not quite so long.' Dovedale Groove was an Extremely Severe route (XS), and for Whillans and Brown the first major Lake District climb of its kind, which Whillans was to follow with Extol (XS) on the same crag in 1960. But Dovedale Groove was the breakthrough. 'In every generation and every decade there's a certain climb that stands out as being more difficult technically than all the other climbs of the same period. They become classic climbs and they never lose their interest. The climb may be noted by the rock character, the technical difficulty, or a combination of both.' Then, said Whillans, 'there's the seriousness of the climb as seen against other climbs – people were generally unprepared to tackle such routes at that stage in the development of rock climbing – so the climb becomes a breakthrough. Like Bill Peascod's Eagle Front, a climb in advance of its period, so to speak. Our climb, Dovedale Groove, got a reputation for technical difficulty. A lot of top climbers tried for years, and weren't able to repeat it, and anyway Dove Crag is in a remote spot and people don't bother to walk up to it.' In fact it was nine years before it was repeated, by Pete Crew and Baz Ingle.

But what do the grades really mean when faced with a crag you have got to climb? After all, surely it is relative, and depends on the weather, the condition of the rock, and the climber – what is 'Severe' for a tall climber might be Very Severe for a climber with small stature and short arms. It is true that one man's climb is another's desperate struggle, so the grades cannot be regarded as absolute, but are reasonably descriptive of their difficulty. *Easy* means a scramble up ledges and sloping rock, where you will probably need a rope. *Moderate* climbs have generous and accessible foot and handholds on sloping rock; *Difficult*, means fairly steep climbing, but with available natural belays (plenty of spikes for a runner), several pitches; *Very Difficult* sorts the climbers from the novices, and requires knowledge of such techniques as jamming, mantleshelfing, bridging; *Severe* climbs have long pitches, and need strenuous climbing; *Very Severe* means you may have to climb in your socks, use techniques like the layback, and worry that you might not make it. *Hard Very Severe* merely compounds the problems encountered on VS; *Extremely Severe* climbs have long and sustained pitches,

Scafell and Wasdale, after a century the area is still the most popular climbing centre in the Lake District. (ICL)

minimal holds, fearsome overhangs, few belay points for protection and require advanced climbing techniques – such was Dovedale Groove.

It takes the climber well over an hour to walk from the Brotherswater Hotel to reach Dove Crag in Dovedale, a crag that was described as having 'one of the steepest cliffs in England ... where it is possible to lie on the very edge and drop a stone straight on to the scree 300 feet below.' The first route up Dove Crag was Westmoreland's Route led by Colonel Horace Westmoreland in 1910. Then came Jim Birkett's Taurus of 1937, but the first major route on the crag was put up by J.W. Haggas who called it Hangover, not on account of the way he felt at the time, but owing to the crag's fiercely overhanging buttress, about twelve feet from the vertical, and just the sort of challenge Whillans enjoys. 'I'm not sure how Dove Crag came to our notice, but once I'd visited it I was very impressed by its height, and because it was all very dark and sombre and mysterious. I'm fairly sure it was me who pointed out the line, and it was the overhanging section that drew our attention to the climb. I thought it might give us a bit of a problem.'

When Chris Bonington and Don Whillans arrived last year to climb the Groove for the Border Television camera crew – for Whillans a gap of some thirty-five years – Bonington stared up at the route in disbelief. 'Is this it, Don?' he said.

'Aye, this is it,' Whillans replied.

'What, up that groove there?' said Bonington in understandable alarm.

'Aye,' said Whillans imperturbably.

'God,' said Bonington, 'It looks absolutely bloody desperate, doesn't it?' But Joe Brown, who did the original climb with Whillans, couldn't even remember it. Brown, on his own admission, never really remembers his climbs unless they are 'epics' involving serious problems. Recently, Whillans asked Brown, 'Do you remember Dovedale Groove, Joe?'

'No,' Brown replied, 'who did you do it with?'

'With you, yer silly bugger,' Whillans growled.

Apart from Hangover, Dove Crag was virtually virgin territory, and this as much as anything must have attracted Whillans – there was plenty of scope for some hard, new routes. As Whillans put it, 'It was obvious that there was a lot of untouched rock, and it was equally obvious that none of the lines was going to be easy – they'd all be harder than Hangover, and that was graded VS.'

Some of the climbs may have been hard, but they were not without their funny side although the following sounds more like a spectator sport: '... water was flushing down my sleeves and running out the bottom of one trouser leg and out of a tear at the top of the other leg. Talk about brass monkeys. Joe had had enough by this time too, his nose was like a road-mender's lamp and his fags were all damp . . . and that was the end of 1951. It went out like a wet firework.'

Brown and Whillans travelled to Dovedale on their motorbikes and camped by a small stone bridge. 'I think we got more out of it than people do today – things are laid on plates for them – but we made a big effort to get up to the Lakes or to Skye. There was no door-to-door transport and no accommodation. We used to climb in winter and sometimes Easter, and we used to get off the bike frozen stiff, pitch the tent in a soggy bog and lie in our wet motorbike clothes. We didn't even have a ground sheet, you know.'

Neither did they have a rucksack. Just a few nylon line slings, a small peg hammer for cleaning out cracks, and the hawser laid nylon rope that had been developed, during the war, for towing gliders. I saved for months to buy that rope, then a stone came down and chopped it in half. Ha, ha!'

They climbed in Woolworth gym shoes, and their protection was from spiked runners and karabiners. A 'spiked runner' is simply a nylon or rope sling, joined by a double fisherman's bend knot, and placed over a spike of rock. The sling would support a karabiner through which the rope would run. But the rope was stiff and developed kinks that could lift the sling off the spike if you were not careful. They also had another type of running belay using pebbles for chockstones. 'You just walked to the foot of the crag and picked up a few suitable looking pebbles off the scree.' These you slipped into cracks in the rock, passed rope slings around them to serve as a belay. The pebble jammed tight and held the sling and karabiner, or 'krab'.

In October of 1953 Whillans did the Girdle of Deer Bield Crag, graded as Extremely Severe (XS,) with two consecutive 75 foot pitches, and perhaps inspired by A.R. Dolphin's magnificent assault of the 'impossible' Deer Bield Buttress, in 1951. But Whillans had other things in mind – the Alps.

In 1952 the Rock and Ice boys headed for Chamonix, and here Whillans had the same sort of revelatory experience that Bill Peascod mentioned in the last chapter. Said Whillans, 'We stayed for ages, looking across first at the slender orange and brown spire of the Dru and then at the great bulk of the Grandes Jorasses. Then I had one of these moments when suddenly everything becomes clear to you. I knew then that I was going to dedicate my life to climbing the hardest and most inaccessible mountains in the world.'

At the foot of the Dru, Whillans met Chris Bonington for the first time. For Bonington, Whillans was 'the best climbing partner I've ever had'. Whillans was hard, very self-disciplined, stocky and obdurate. Bonington,

on the other hand, was tall, untidy, somewhat changeable, often disorganised, and with what Whillans described as a 'plum in the gob' voice. They
were a great team in the mountains, but had less in common at ground
level. 'Chris falls between the ship and the dock – he has a genuine love of
mountains and enjoys climbing, but it's fifty-fifty with him because of the
course he's taken and his income depends on it. He's very well aware of his
public image, and he is climbing as well as he ever did – or nearly as well.
The trouble is he has to do all this training nonsense now to keep up with
the others. I would put Chris as a very fine all-round mountaineer, he
rock-climbs well and is very good in the big mountains.' And Whillans adds,
with faint cynicism, 'He must have made an awful lot of money out of it.'
In Whillans' day, a mountaineer usually returned from an expedition in
debt. If he was lucky he just about broke even, and 'to make a few quid was
the ultimate success.' Then, torn between his dislike of the commercialism, and
his respect for Bonington's ability, Whillans says, 'Apart from Joe, Chris was
the best I've ever climbed with.' And he added 'I'd trust me life wi' Chris.'

Bonington recalled their first meeting in 1958: 'We watched the two
figures come closer, the foremost, cloth-cap on his head, was short and
powerfully muscled – it was Don Whillans all right.' Bonington was privi-
ledged to then witness Whillans' prowess on the rock. 'He started the pitch
with a magnificent display of climbing. He did not hurry: each move was
smooth, calculated and seemingly effortless, and yet, when I came to follow,
the rock thrust me backwards. At the end of the overhang Don had swung
across a steep slab on the rope clipped to a peg above him, and had van-
ished. I followed, and found myself in a bottomless groove. Looking down,
the first thing I saw was the glacier 2,000 feet below. Far above, quite
unattainable, a pair of legs were swinging in the air. A crack, smooth, sheer,
unadorned with pitons or wedges, stretched upwards; it was barred by two
small overhangs.

'Did you go up there?' I shouted at the legs.

'Yes,' came a voice.

'Is it hard?' I asked.

'It's a bit strenuous,' came the reply, in a flat Lancashire accent, and the
legs kicked idly against the rock.'

Don Whillans had, and still has, tremendous confidence but a shrewd
realist's sense of proportion: 'Look, I've got a long list of mates who are dead
– not just a few. Today, the young lads, when I see them soloing some of
the hardest climbs it really does make me cringe, because I know that
anything can happen at any given second. I've seen them soloing and looking

safe, but anything can bloody happen – suddenly one of them would be off that rock and he'd be smashed to bits down there – end of story. I can appreciate the skill and nerve of the fellows doing it, but I don't like watching it.' Whillans is like an old soldier who has lost his taste for the fight, or is no longer prepared to accept the sacrifice. 'Like when Chris and I were on the Central Tower of Paine and the rope snapped. He was just hovering. The rope snapped, he fell down, landed on this ledge with all this loose rock, and he rolled down the ledge to the brink. He was actually standing on his head with the rucksack pulling him over with a big drop into the gully, a thousand feet below. He was just kicking his legs in the air, and I thought "If he goes that way it's the end of story, and if he comes this way he'll be all right", and he just went the right way ... Things like that happen the whole time in climbing.' Whillans should know. He climbed Everest with the International Expedition in 1971 and was then reckoned to be Britain's finest all-round mountaineer. He had spent a punishing eight weeks at above 23,000 feet and got to within spitting distance of the Masherbrum summit in 1957 when his companion collapsed, and one of the team, Bob Downes, died. But he did make the summit of Annapurna, during the Bonington Expedition of 1970 when Ian Clough was killed by a falling serac – a tower of ice – during the descent. Whillans has seen it all. He brought the Indian mountaineer, Harsh Baghuna, frozen to death, down from below Everest's summit, and he is critical of bold, impetuous climbers who, as Whillans sees it, take unnecessary risks. 'Doug Scott – now he's another one. I've said to him more than once – listen, mate, you're living on borrowed time.' With Mick Burke, Tom Patey and Dougal Haston gone, there are precious few left.

Don Whillans reserves most of his contempt for what he sees as the new, competitive and publicity-seeking element in the climbing world, and especially among rock climbers. 'This is what happens: we had a friend who was a climber, and he was an intensely competitive person. He was in the same club as me and Joe, but he wouldn't climb with us in case he didn't get credit for anything he did, in case we stole the bloody limelight. That's what he actually said! I thought he was bloody joking, me, 'cos in those days you went for the crack and the camping, and you enjoyed the atmosphere – it was the atmosphere that was great! This obviously didn't mean much to him, and he gave up climbing, quite suddenly. They're all the same these people. The minute they're not the best, and right at the top, they give it up. Pete Livesey has bloody given it up now. Livesey's honest enough to admit it – but most of them won't even say that. Being competitive to that extent is a sure sign that there's something not quite right in yer 'ed for my money . . .'

It is obvious that Whillans would like to be back in the fray, right at the top as he once was, leading the Extremely Severe routes up the rocks with Joe Brown, and in the mountains with Bonington. A conservative and a traditionalist, Whillans was also very competitive as are all climbers, but he never allowed competitiveness to cloud his judgement in the mountains. He has retained a deep respect for the ethics of climbing in which, as he sees it, athletics have no place and 'sport' is the wrong label.

'Sport is a wrong word to describe what climbing is about, or *was* about. You spent all weekend doing it. There was no real competition. You didn't race against another feller. It's more serious than "pastime" since you can get killed doing it, especially in the mountains. You get these fanatical, competitive nutters who really aren't climbers or mountaineers deep down. They are actually competitive people who drift into climbing, and for a while they're at the top of the tree, writing articles and all this – then they're gone! I recognise them for what they are – and they are not people who actually love mountains. A lot of these lads wouldn't dream of going and climbing remote mountains in the Himalayas or in China, because they'd be out there and nobody's ever going to see them for donkey's years, but they want their climbs to be in the magazines, in a month's time – some little bit of rock they've climbed; they've never bivouacked in a storm, or climbed a rock that's covered in ice!'

Rock climbing, once preparatory to climbing the 'big mountains', is now a highly-specialised activity where mountaineering is scornfully referred to as 'snow bashing' as one might compare a racehorse to a cart-horse. Well, is this snow bashing?: 'From the first touch I knew it was going to be a supreme test of my skill and strength. The sun was now full on the gully and it was stifling inside our wind-proofed, padded clothing. I sweated my way up the rock, oblivious to everything except the few feet ahead. I banged in pitons and hung from them, gasping for breath for minutes on end, my heart thumping and sweat blinding me.

Carefully, I cut steps in the tough ice until I was perched on the top of the tongue, my hands grasping the underside of the flake. This was it: a strenuous layback in high-altitude gear at 25,000 feet. I moved as swiftly as I could, fighting my way up.

'Bastard!' I gasped as I made the discovery that the top of the crack was jammed with ice.

But I had burned my boats, I had to get up, a fall would mean an injury and that would do for both of us. I made a desperate heave and somehow pulled up on to a small, ice-covered ledge on top of the flake. I lay panting, waiting for strength to return to return to my body.'

That was Whillans and Joe Walmsley on Masherbrum in the Himalayas. A 'layback', by the way, is a climbing technique: imagine the corner of a room, and where the walls meet there's a vertical crack wide enough for your fingers. Stretch out your arms and grab the crack with both hands, close together. Now walk up the wall until your feet meet your hands so you are pushing with your feet, pulling with your hands, and your body, bent like a hairpin, is suspended above the ground. Now move up the crack to reach the ceiling. Try to imagine executing this while wearing a flying suit, at 25,000 feet and you might begin to understand why a not insignificant proportion of the population discover that mountaineering is not for them.

Mountaineering is more dangerous than rock climbing. Hidden crevasses, falling seracs and sudden avalanches take their toll, not to mention mountain sickness and other hazards. There are more fatalities on the snow slopes, and it is clear that Whillans still regards the crags as the preparatory school for the big mountains so that, if climbing is to be taken seriously, you progress from the crags to the high peaks; your skill on the rock is really put to the test on the ice walls. This was the classic approach, but the mountains are no longer the ultimate goal. The early pioneers such as Jones and Herford had a natural aptitude for rock-climbing coupled with a passion for seeking difficult climbs which allowed them to test their ability and endurance – a contest, in fact, between the climber and the crag or mountain. Actually Jones had more in common with Peter Livesey than with Whillans. Jones and Livesey are technical, scientific climbers, more concerned with their physical reaction to the rock, than to the spirit of mountaineering and the aesthetic appeal. It was the Age of Discovery, of the Lakes and fells and also of the sport itself. It was also an age of innocence and amateurism. With the appearance of Whillans and Brown in the 1950s, the link between the crags and the peaks was continued (more in Whillans' case than in Joe Brown's) and the sport of rock-climbing advanced significantly. Their hard routes presaged the future. Climbers were still discovering unclimbed crags, but a new approach was beginning to develop where strategy and technique were employed, where fewer available routes meant a more competitive outlook. Whillans, whose sympathies are with the early romanticists, would prefer that the ethic of amateurism prevailed; the routes that Whillans put up were for the sport – personal recognition was incidental.

Climbers have always received recognition for pioneering routes and pushing forward the frontiers, but in the late 1960s an abrasive competitiveness began to be evident among climbers; perhaps it had always been there, subliminally. Rock-climbing was still basically a contest between the rock and the climber, but a hard-headed egocentricity had emerged, where routes of extreme risk and difficulty were measures of individual superiority, not only over the rock, but over one's fellow climbers. It was the Age of the By-line. Once having acquired this attitude, it is difficult to return to v-diffs and VSs.

This attitude didn't seem to affect mountaineers in quite the same way. True, the exploits of Hillary, Hunt, Bonington, Bonatti, Messner and others had put them on the front page from time to time. There was also great competition between climbers on an expedition to be among those to go for the summit, but a man who has stood on top of the Eiger or Mont Blanc seems to acquire a more philosophical, complacent view of climbing. Perhaps mountaineers feel so superior that they wish to disassociate themselves from the 'nit-picking' as Whillans calls it. 'I can't even be bothered talking to half of them, because they've got down to such nit-picking now, because a lot of the rocks have been climbed. At one time the main interest was in *exploration*. You'd go to new crags, or crags that had only a few climbs on them. But now they've come to the athlete bit – and the athlete bit is now more important than the bloody rock bit!' Of course, what really upsets Whillans is the lost innocence, the halcyon days of the pebble chock-stones and the hemp rope; the 'crack and the camping' are still there, but there isn't a lot left to explore.

Over the years Whillans has mellowed (slightly) and he has put on a lot of weight which his old friend Nat Allen is at a loss to understand. 'Everest may have affected Don's metabolism in some way. He doesn't eat all that much, and okay – he drinks, but that shouldn't really put him at fourteen stone from a mere seven or eight stone.'

The weight has certainly curtailed his climbing activities, at least on the hard routes. Some say he has given up entirely.

'I'm thinking of going to the Dolomites or the Pyrenees next summer. I'll probably go with one of the old Rock and Ice Club fellows called Harry Smith, who is still climbing well. We want to do classic climbs, climbs of great character and a fair standard of difficulty – the modern climbs would be too hard for us, and wouldn't have the appeal.' Well, last year he managed to climb his classic Dovedale Groove for the Border Television cameras but, as he said at the time, 'it was bloody hard, but the top part which many people regard as the hardest pitch, because it's an overhanging crack on a chimney, I can actually take quite a lot of my body weight off my hands. That's the type of climbing I used to do. I could reduce my body weight by getting my shoulder in the crack and leaning my backside on a wall of rock. Other people I know find it very hard, that.'

Whillans and Brown are still climbing, though Whillans has now joined the lecture tour circuit, but he is free to enjoy the aspect of climbing that he most loves – the company he keeps: 'The climb isn't *the* main thing, it's only half of it. The rest is being in the mountains and the company that I'm in. For the most part of my climbing life, not the early years of course, but most of it, there's always been a pint and seeing other climbers in the pub and a few stories – that's the *real* climbing scene that's kept me so long in it.'

Chris Bonington, mountaineer, expedition leader, and rock-climber, photographed just after his 50th birthday. He still climbs with 'an enormous enthusiasm that verges on mania'. (AB)

4

Chris Bonington: Holy Ghost

Chris Bonington, CBE, is the first mountaineer to acquire that glossy, international superstar status enjoyed by footballers, racing drivers and tennis players. He is recognised almost everywhere he goes – even by those who are not too sure what he is famous for. While other climbers have had fame thrust upon them for one spectacular deed – Hillary and Tenzing for the conquest of Everest in 1953, Messner and Habeler, the first to climb Everest without oxygen – Bonington's reputation is the outcome of a long-term investment in consistent climbing. Bonington has dedicated thirty-five years to climbing and within that time has captured the public's imagination through a series of bold adventures.

Moreover, he has skilfully presented the conservative world of mountaineering and rock-climbing to the mass media, with himself as both interpreter and enthusiastic protagonist. He is a superb communicator, making his television debut in 1965 when pioneering a route up the High Rock in Cheddar Gorge for an ITV outside broadcast. He was the first climber to stand on top of the Old Man of Hoy in the Orkney Islands, repeating the climb for the cameras. In the summer of 1984 he climbed again for film crews, reviewing a number of historic Lakeland climbs for Border Television and Channel 4.

Now aged fifty, Bonington is still climbing with 'an enormous enthusiasm that verges on a mania – it blocks out everything else.' In 1983, Jim Fotheringham, a fellow Cumbrian and mountaineer, pioneered with Bonington a new route up the 21,000-foot Shivling in the Himalayas, climbing up to the top and down the other side in six days. 'He's a complete addict who gets carried away by the sheer immediacy of the venture. Wherever he finds himself,' said Fotheringham, wonderingly, 'whether away on a lecture tour or staying with friends, Chris manages to get a climb in. It

Chris Bonington and Mike Thompson, an anthropologist and mountaineer, who was with Bonington on Annapurna and Everest (BT)

Right Bonington and Thompson on Scafell in 1984, nearly twenty years after they put up their 'near miss' climb, Holy Ghost. (BT)

doesn't matter if it's thirty feet or three hundred feet, even a stone wall will do ...'

There is no doubt that Chris Bonington's physical appearance has contributed something to his success. It is easy to feel that he could be a character in a Norse saga, capable of epic deeds and adventures, a legacy, perhaps, of his Danish ancestry. Photographs of Bonington in his mid-twenties show a clean-shaven, good-looking young man with full lips, a straight nose and a faintly quizzical expression. Maturity has added a rangy leanness but the youthful vigour remains. He is now tall and tousled and weathered, and the full beard is streaked with grey.

Mike Thompson, an anthropologist, who climbed on Annapurna South Face with Bonington in 1970, and joined him on the 1975 Everest expedition, first met him in the army and remembers the fresh-faced lad with the confident Sandhurst voice, which has since acquired a north country inflexion. Whillans referred to Bonington as 'a public school climber' – a significant social comment in the climbing world there, until recent times, *all* climbers were public schoolboys, and the likes of Whillans were rare. The Rock and Ice boys grinned at the mention of Bonington – but that was before they had seen him in action.

Bonington, decided Whillans, was a fine mountaineer: 'We were an ill-assorted pair, but we balanced each other – his impetuosity, my stolidness; his volubility, my terseness. On a climb we made a sound partnership and I enjoyed climbing with him immensely. If Joe wasn't here, I could think of nobody better to share the climb with than Chris.'

Christian Bonington was born in London in 1934, and educated at University College School in Hampstead. His parents had separated when Bonington was a year old, a somewhat rare event in those days, with the result that he bore a feeling of inferiority at school, where he was shy and not especially popular.

'I suppose I was encouraged, in some ways, to be a loner. My mother had to go out to work and in my school holidays I was mainly on my own, although she sent me to farm camps and places like that. As I got older I went cycling and adventure-wandering. It was during a cycling holiday that I first saw the Welsh hills and thought 'Gosh! it would be terrific to walk among them.' In the early winter of 1951 I hitch-hiked to Snowdonia and watched people rock-climbing, and I knew instinctively that here was something I'd like to have a go at.'

A friend of Bonington's family took him to Harrison's Rocks near Tunbridge Wells, the climber's equivalent of a skier's nursery slopes. It was here

The Medlar, a route put up by Bonington and Martin Boysen on Raven Crag, Thirlmere. The climb, rated E3, takes its name from a Medlar Tree in the cave at the start of the route. (CB)

Bonington pondering on the difficulties that lie ahead on the route Footless Crow, Borrowdale. (AB).

Left Bonington on 'The Gibbet', a climb with a single pitch of 110', on Recastle Crag, Watendlath. (CB).

that Bonington became totally hooked on climbing. 'I knew I had found a pursuit that I loved, that my body and temperament seemed designed for it, and that I was happy.' He loves climbing with a deep and passionate intensity which he conveys with an infectious fervour. He is really relaxed and happy only in the climbing environment or at home with his wife Wendy. Yet he has never belonged to the cliquey circle of his generation, Don Whillans and the 'lads in the pub'. Bonington's public image seems partly to be the reason, and it clashes with the conservative attitudes of the climbing fraternity. Climbers are like jazz musicians, introspective and solitary, relaxed only with their own kind, and who perform more for themselves and their peers than for public approbation.

'Chris wants to be one of the lads,' explained Jim Fotheringham, who isn't exactly one of the lads himself, 'but they won't let him. He isn't really a drinker, nor is he a very sociable character, although he has developed a veneer of sociability that copes okay.'

Bonington has, however, a wonderful facility for describing this world of 'running belays', 'jumar clamps', 'karabiners' and 'descendeurs' and sudden death, and his books have become best-sellers. He is honest about his climbing status: 'I suppose in the late 1950s and early 1960s I was among the top ten to fifteen rock climbers, but I was never right at the top, like Don. I think that my greatest abilities have been in alpinism, in Himalayas climbing and particularly in expedition leadership and organisation.'

Everest expeditions generate a predictable series of emotional reactions among climbers in the team. Everyone wants to be among the chosen few to push for the summit. Climbers may then reveal *prima donna* tendencies in the competitive atmosphere, and squabbling and backbiting are not entirely unknown when zero temperatures and shrieking winds put everyone under heavy strain. Personal habits then become targets for sharp criticism and comment. Despite enjoying organization, Bonington, on his own admission, can be slightly lazy and inclined to prefer squalor in preference to order. 'A frightful person to share a tent with,' said Charles Clarke, the doctor on the 1975 Everest expedition.

This view was confirmed by Mike Thompson, who accuses Bonington of being totally disorganised. 'He loses things, is absent-minded, chaotic and unpunctual.' Thompson remembered when Bonington lost a cheque for £50 in his bed, 'and it took two weeks to surface.' Yet Charles Clarke sees Bonington as 'a person of enormous power. He is very convincing, very believable and utterly dedicated. He sustains the plans he has made, and does exactly what he has said he was going to do.' Perhaps his passion for war games ('I am a frustrated Field Marshal') contributes to his flair for organisation and his gift of leadership which, coupled with his natural enthusiasm, carries all before it – like an avalanche. 'At his peak,' said a friend, 'Chris unwittingly trod on a few people.'

The climbing fraternity felt that his fund-raising and publicity-seeking efforts were not always in the true interests of the sport. However, Bonington's steely resolve and single-mindedness were essential to the success of the expedition.

Weighed against charges of arrogance and self-interest are the assertions made by several of Bonington's friends, that he is extremely generous, lovable and loyal. Mike Thompson even found his 'transparent greed' an endearing quality – 'he'll always manage to eat the last of whatever's on the plate "by accident"' Thompson said admiringly, 'then apologise afterwards.' Others discern a darker side to his personality, a vulnerability and underlying sadness, 'and then the shutters come down.'

By all accounts Chris Bonington is climbing as well as he ever did, although inevitably not at the high standard of today's aggressive young climbers. Pete Whillance, one of the team climbing The Old Man of Hoy in front of the television cameras, outlined the hard routine that climbing now demands. 'Modern climbers are just like athletes. They train like athletes and climb eight hours a day, every single day of their lives. The technical standards are continuously going forward, and just like runners the climbers are knocking time off records.'

Climbs are graded according to how technically difficult they are to ascend, and the level of protection they afford, in other words, how far you have to fall before the rope stops you, unless, of course, the rope breaks ... It is clear that climbers feel a sense of triumph at having cheated fate – rather like Russian roulette. It is a drug to the emotions and becomes a habit. 'Climbers,' declared Fotheringham, 'are not a sane bunch of people at all.' When Bonington describes his struggles to surmount a savage overhang above a bottomless void, you wonder if he and all other climbers are not more than slightly crazy. 'God, I've had it,' he shouts as he falls off a 10,000-foot spire or peak in Patagonia. 'Make a mistake now, and you're dead, Bonington,' he mutters to himself on the Eiger. Why do they do it? Partly because the investment of risk and fear and the prospect of a fatality is repaid a hundredfold by the tremendous euphoria and elation at the end of a hard climb. 'A great bubbling wave of joy rolls over me,' Bonington writes, 'I gaze down, across the face, with a rich feeling of contentment. It had been the hardest, and certainly the most spectacular ice pitch I'd

Opposite Bonington leading a route on Black Crag, Borrowdale, in the summer of 1983. (PM)

Jumaring or prussilering is the opposite of abseiling – a means of ascent on a rope using a jumar clamp, a self-locking device incorporating a ratchet. (BT)

Abseiling is a controlled descent on a rope secured from above. Also known as 'rappelling', the inexperienced climber can suffer from severe rope burns if the descent is too rapid. (BT) ever climbed.' Later, in confirmation of the risks involved, Bonington's friend and fellow climber John Harlin plunged 5,000 feet to his death when a fixed rope broke. Bonington the photographer, covering the Eiger climb for the *Telegraph* magazine, located the body but couldn't bring himself to take a picture of it, but Bonington the writer described 'the strange and terrible beauty in the juxtaposition of the bent limbs ... a picture that said everything that could possibly be said about the North Wall of the Eiger.'

Bonington's involvement with the big mountains, and with Himalayan expeditions, has made him famous as a mountaineer in a way that rock climbing never could. Indeed mountaineering has somewhat taken precedence over his first love, however: 'I've always remained an enthusiastic rock climber, and I love climbing in this county.' Bonington has made his home in the Lakes and fully qualifies as a Lakeland climber. He has pioneered several classic routes, particularly in Avon Gorge, though he does not claim to have done the consistent pioneering kind of climbing. According to Martin Boysen, with whom Bonington put up Medlar on Raven Crag in 1964, Bonington is intensely competitive – 'but hides it'. All climbers are competitive in their fashion, but Bonington's competitiveness is tempered by caution and an instict for self-preservation that many top climbers lack – or suppress. If he does not have the simian agility of the rock-gymnasts, he does have a totally honest view of his own abilities, and can write objectively about his successes and his failures. His climb on the East Buttress of Scafell, the route called Holy Ghost, is a better story than it is a climb. He and his companion, Mike Thompson, had grossly underestimated the difficulties which proved a formidable challenge to their courage and resourcefulness.

'Mike was the brains,' said Bonington, 'He's a great "new-router" so he would actually pick out the lines. He would point me out the line and I'd lead it. It was Mike's idea to do the girdle traverse of the East Buttress of Scafell'. When climbers get bored of vertical ascents, they can always go sideways, and this is called traversing. A girdle traverse is a route from one end of a crag to the other, or even right round it. A traverse can be harder and more 'necky' than a straightforward ascent; for one thing the route is longer and incorporates pitches where the climber has to ascend or descend to follow the line of the route. Also, stances and points of protection are often further apart.

'When we set out to do it,' Bonington recalls, 'it was a little too early in the season and bitterly cold. At the time I was living in a furnished house at Woodland, near Broughton in Furness. We had driven across in my mini van to Eskdale and then walked up Eskdale and Mickledore to the East

Buttress. Our main plan was to make a better and full traverse, as the existing route missed out most of the hard parts. We didn't inspect the route first, nor did we garden it – it was absolutely "on sight."' Bonington and Thompson did the climb in 1965, the early days of the 'nut runners'. 'People had started threading ordinary Whitworth nuts of various sizes on to slings, having first drilled out the thread. You'd carry eight or nine slings with a variety of nuts from very small to large – different size nuts for different cracks. You would also have thin line slings with much smaller nuts and a karabiner on each sling. The ropes we used were still hawser laid nylon, but the specialised climbing shoe called EB's were now widely used, and I certainly had a pair.'

The Holy Ghost climb was in effect a non-route, a mistake; they did not really mean to do it. They traversed from the foot of Gremlin's Groove across a steep wall to the foot of a route called Trinity, first put up by Don Whillans, and the intention was then to go rightwards and down to Hell's Groove. This second pitch went round a steep corner, on to a prow of rock and straight up to an overhang. 'Then you had to go round the overhang and by that time I was about fifteen feet from my belay. I set off with a blithe optimism up to this vertical nose where there was a foothold and then a series of undercuts. At that point I was going into a corner and had no idea what was on the other side. The holds were all rounded and I remember going up them in a blind sweat.' At this point Bonington was committed, and had made some irreversible moves. There is a stage in many climbs where you reach the point of no return, when you are 'committed,' and you are obliged to go forward whatever the outcome, unless you can climb down. Climbing is thus a philosophy of total commitment and progressive achievement, of bravado and competitiveness and, as Bill Peascod said, 'bloody ego'. 'I was dead frightened when I realised I couldn't retreat. I got round the corner but there was no easy ledge to go for, and nothing to hang on to. So it was a blind alley and I'd had it, and the only thing I could have done was to jump off.'

This is the sort of situation every climber dreads next to falling off. There you are, with thirty feet of rope out, clinging to the rock and unable to move in any direction. The only thing you can do is call for a top rope, secured from above so that you can climb up it to safety. 'At this stage my courage had run out, and when I saw a group of people passing below I called down to ask them for a top rope. They were, in fact, three young soldiers who were not climbers, but they carried on to the foot of the crag and shouted up to a party who were climbing a route called Mickledore

Groove, saying that there were some people in trouble and they wanted a top rope. One of the climbers was John Wilkinson, later President of the Fell and Rock, but they were halfway up their climb, so I had to wait.'

'If you are in a frightening situation,' advises the climber Peter Livesey, 'you've got to force yourself to think about the climb.' Bonington's courage gradually returned while he was waiting for Wilkinson and the top rope, 'I managed to get a good nut in at floor level, then I started looking around and saw that going upwards – though it was very steep – there were some small holds, and I thought "I can climb out of this". It was hard going for another twenty feet to a decent stance. Then I bought Mike up, and he had quite a struggle getting up as well.' Bonington and Thompson climbed straight up to the top of the crag, and decided that the route was 'as hard and necky as any climb that had yet been done in the Lake District. We called the climb Holy Ghost because it was next door to Whillans' Trinity, and we were so bloody frightened.'

Historically the route is interesting because it opened up the girdle traverse later to be known as The Lord of the Rings, of which Holy Ghost is the crux pitch. 'The line of the traverse just drops away and looks horrendous, and we'd have had to go down that.' In 1969 two Lakeland climbers, Colin Reade and John Adams, did go down it. They took two days to complete the traverse, which includes something like nineteen pitches during 1200 feet of climbing. Then in 1974, Pete Livesey did the first solo.

In 1983, with the benefit of past experience, if not of the passing years, Chris Bonington returned to Scafell to try the Lord of the Rings traverse. 'I went with a very good climber and he failed on it. Then I freaked out and failed on it, then I went back a couple of weeks later and actually climbed it – The Lord of the Rings is a beautiful and classic route.' Obviously, age tempers one's ardour for the hard and the necky climbs, especially at altitude in the Alps or the Himalayas, and you have to pace yourself.

Bonington, who began as a fledgeling climber on Harrison's Rocks, and graduated on the Lakeland Crags, followed in the classic tradition of the early pioneers. After the Eiger and Mont Blanc, Bonington reached the summit of his career on Annapurna and Everest. Well, almost – but not quite. Surprisingly, Bonington the Everest Expedition leader has never set foot on the summit, although he has been very close to it. Climbing to Camp 6 on the 1975 Expedition, Bonington reached 27,300 feet, with a mere 1728 feet to go to the top, but as leader it was not his place to join the assault team – Haston and Scott went instead.

In 1985, however, Bonington will go to Everest not as leader but as a member of the team. 'I'd like to go for the summit, and I think the chances are pretty good and I'm fit enough for my age. The big problems will be the wind, the cold, the lack of oxygen, and the fact that your body is actually physically deteriorating at that altitude. But you have to spend some time in these conditions in order to become acclimatized. So you have two conflicting things – the deterioration and the acclimatization. If you go up too fast, there's a risk of mountain sickness, but if you go up too slowly, you have the problem of deterioration and you haven't the strength to get to the top.' Don Whillans, who went with the 1971 International Expedition, and has not stood on Everest's summit either, described the effect of altitude on a *Sunday Times* journalist who barely had the strength to stand. 'He'd walk six feet, then he had to sit down. The poor bugger spent the whole time sitting in his tent!'

'As you get into your late forties,' Bonington explained, 'your rate of recovery is slower and you get really exhausted. Say I have one attempt and I fail, the probability is on a single trip that I wouldn't recover, whereas in my thirties I could have gone down, rested for a week, and then have had a second attempt.' Martin Boysen, who went with Bonington to Annapurna, pointed out that 'any climber who has any pretensions wants to stand on the highest point in the world.' For Bonington, who received his CBE for services to British mountaineering, the desire to reach the top is 'a little itch. No, actually it's a big itch.' About a hundred and fifty people have successfully climbed the world's highest mountain, including several women climbers. 'I don't care if I'm the hundred and sixtieth person, so long as I get there. Anyway, it will be a nice view from the top.'

5

Pete Livesey: Footless Crow

In the early 1970s a term was added to the climber's vocabulary. The new generation of rock climbers were called 'rock-athletes'. In fact the term was not absolutely new. In the 1950s the very pushy climbers were described as 'rock-gymnasts'. O.G. Jones was a rock gymnast and so was Don Whillans, and Arthur Dolphin, men as fluid and flexible on the rock as a virtuoso's fingers on the keyboard. The word 'athlete', however, was timely and apposite and recalled the Olympic ideal. An athlete is a *competitor*, while a gymnast is a practitioner. The new kind of climber who has succeeded Whillans and Bonington reflects the inevitable fact that rock-climbing can never get any easier, it can only get more difficult. 'The word "athelete" is for real now. At one time it was a joke amongst the climbing world,' said Whillans caustically. 'The scene has changed so that now there are people who are doing it for quite different reasons.'

In the bleak and discordant seventies putting up hard routes became a serious matter. Another new term was coined by rock-athletes. They called themselves 'activists' – a political word which implied a ruthlessness similar to that adopted by some political groups. As a group, the activists were inspired by the example and unique professional approach of Peter Livesey. Although Livesey was relatively unknown he had, in fact, been climbing since he was fifteen. Livesey kept a low profile in the climbing world until at the age of thirty-one, he began to put up the magnificent new routes for which he became famous.

Like Bill Peascod, Livesey climbed alone at first, just scrambling around in quarries. 'I didn't know anything about climbing, and a rope therefore wouldn't have helped me much. Then I became a caver, so by the time I came into regular climbing I had a strong start – I didn't begin from scratch, as it were. I realised that I was climbing at almost the top standard of the day without doing anything at all – just by climbing.' Peter Livesey was born in Huddersfield, Yorkshire, in 1943, the eldest of three children. His father was a builder's merchant, his mother a school teacher. Livesey was educated at a local grammar school where he quickly showed promise in athletics becoming a Junior International cross-country runner. Later he became a first rate canoeist. Now aged forty-one, Livesey has the bearing of the lean academic, slightly stooping and bespectacled. He has an abundance of fine curly hair, unruly and now turning grey. He lectures on recreation, leisure studies and outdoor activities at Ilkley College, and has recently taken up competitive fell-running. Yet there is little outward evidence of this seemingly endless source of energy. Livesey is, by all accounts, a very complex character and difficult to get to know. 'Cryptic,' says his one time climbing partner Jill Lawrence. John Sheard, with whom Livesey did some very hard and famous climbs, said that Livesey is extremely calculating and methodical, although to the casual observer he comes across as being disorganised. Relationships are entered into judiciously and warily: he tests people, seeing how far he can push or stretch the bounds of tolerance, much as he might test himself on the rock-face. Perhaps somewhere at a subliminal level he distrusts people and situations – people are guilty until proved innocent. He will not suffer fools gladly, being impatient with ditherers since he always knows what he wants to do, knows where he is going, and rarely expresses self-doubt. 'A lot of people think he's pretty brash,' said Jill Lawrence, 'and he is egocentric, but perhaps to be that successful in anything, you have to be.'

When the American climber Henry Barber came to Britain, he saw Livesey as a 'wild-looking, egocentric combatant.' Barber's arrival, and his reputation, seems to have kindled an intensely competitive reaction in Livesey. Barber, some ten years Livesey's junior, was an unknown quantity, and perhaps a potential threat to his status. Livesey's remarkable climbing career – the preparation, planning, trial period and final public demonstration – shows his methodical mind and his competitive attitude. Said Jill Lawrence, 'Pete's an achiever. He likes to succeed at things, to the extent, say, that he wouldn't bother to start something if he felt he wasn't going to be a success at it – not just a mediocre success – but at a high level. Peter doesn't express personal doubts about things, I'm sure doubts go through his mind, but he doesn't communicate them. Yet, on the other hand, he is a very gentle, caring sort of person.'

Many climbers are competitive, athletic and achievers, but they do not all climb like Livesey. 'He undoubtedly increased climbing standards,' Pete

85

Derwent Water from Goat Crag, Borrowdale, an area first explored by the Abrahams, the 'Keswick Brothers' in the 1890's. (AB)

Pete Livesey, the rock-athlete of the 1970's and forerunner of today's 'activists'. Livesey's rigorous training programme plus his great flair enabled him to create climbs of hitherto unimagined difficulty, and to set new standards of grading. (JS)

87

Willance explained, 'but it was done more through his approach. He adopted a new approach, a fierce attitude to climbing that hadn't really been taken before. He also took what some people think of as a ruthless attitude towards the sport. He prepared his routes very carefully so that he knew exactly what he was doing before he started.'

Sheard thinks that what made Livesey different was the degree of risk that he was prepared to accept, but Livesey believes the risk was limited since he knew exactly what he was doing, and just how far he could push it, following Peascod's and Whillans' technique of climbing just below their own limits and capabilities.

Livesey applies to his climbing an analytical, investigative approach to his own physical dynamics and mental stability and endurance. He is equally thorough in his study of the rock to be climbed. He saw the unexplored territories of rock, and where frontiers needed to be advanced at a time when rock-climbing had reached an impasse and awaited a fresh spark of inspiration. Livesey was to provide that inspiration, seeing what could still be achieved, and he knew that he was the person to achieve it. Tremendously self-confident of his own physical skill and strong psychological security, he practically dispensed with protection.

'When I first started climbing I soloed everything, you see. Although I had a rope I did'nt put in any protection at all. I never had any equipment either, and virtually everything I climbed I was prepared to go solo.' Livesey speaks rapidly with the occasional hesitant stutter, relieved by contemplative pauses. 'I knew what I was doing, I would be taking risks only if I didn't know what I was doing, so I was probably technically climbing below my natural capabilities.'

The rock face, be it gritstone, limestone or volcanic rhyolite, is a set proving ground for each climber's physical and mental stamina. Much that is perhaps latent in the individual finds expression and realisation on the surface of the rock. The more it defies one's attempts to ascend, the more it draws from the climber his own special talents or confirms a lack of them. Until Livesey had shown the way ahead with his route Footless Crow, most climbers had failed on crags where there were long, sustained pitches with little opportunity for rest or protection. 'Sustained pitches' are stretches of rock, usually sheer walls on an incline, a long way from the ground, where there are few resting places or stances for a belay. The progress of your ascent relies largely on your fingers and arms, there is nowhere that you can rest on your feet. What you can do is rest by hanging on to a running belay, but this is unacceptable to purists since, in effect, it divides the pitch into two separate pitches as the runner then becomes a stance. On a sustained pitch your arms get tired and there's no time to stop and place protection (nut runners) in cracks – if there are any cracks – or place slings over spikes of rock. Furthermore, the long pitch means that you are carrying the weight of a lot of rope which adds weight to your body as you climb, especially on overhangs. Footless Crow is a prime example of a long, sustained and strenuous pitch, and was graded as Extremely Severe (E5). Today, with the advanced forms of protection available, Footless Crow would only rate an E4, but as every climber knows, grades are all relative to the individual performance and pitches can vary considerably in difficulty and risk throughout the climb. The crux pitch of Footless Crow is incredibly hard and strenuous but to many of today's climbers it represents a mere 'ten foot wonder'.

When Livesey completed his routes, in the summer of 1974, he realised that current grades were unrealistic since his climbs were harder than anything previously attempted. In an article published in Mountain magazine, he suggested refining the Extremely Severe grade into subdivisions of Mild, Standard, Hard, and 'even harder'. The Lakeland climber Peter Botterill (no relation to the Botterill of Botterill's Slab) then came up with the idea of numerical progression. 'An Extremely Severe,' he said, 'should be graded as E1, E2, E3, and so on.' The idea was not new. A group of climbers had suggested classification by numbers, in the 1940s. This plan was attacked by the conservative fraternity as being too scientific, and was subsequently dropped, but by the 1970s a more accurate system was needed. Botterill's plan was snatched, while still warm, by his rival the South Lakes climber Ed Cleasby, who suggested grading all the Lake District climbs accordingly.

An article by Cleasby appeared in *Crags Magazine* in 1976, and the system later gained the approval of the Fell and Rock Climbing Club. The climbs that followed Footless Crow were Nagasaki Grooves and Dry Grasp, both E4's, and Bitter Oasis, E3. Two years later Pete Botterill, inspired by the New Order, added his own E4 route called, appropriately, 'Masochist'.

It was now possible to apply these standards to early climbs. Thus Brown and Whillans' Dovedale Groove is now an E1; Jim Birkett's Harlot Face of 1949 is an E1, although Very Severe was the only top grading at the time, some of Dolphin's climbs are graded E1 today, and several of Allan Austin's rate an E2. As a matter of historical interest, there's a route called Suicide Wall, put up in 1945, that has now been graded an E2, while Jack Long-

89

Girdled with an assortment of chocks, karabiners, friends, and a bag of chalk, Livesey allows himself the rare luxury of advanced protection as he prepares to climb Goat Crag. (AB)

Pete Livesey leading on his famous route 'Footless Crow' on Goat Crag, Borrowdale, ten years after he pioneered it in 1974. Chris Bonington is belaying from a stance below. (AB)

land's (now Sir Jack Longland) climb Javelin Blade on Idwal Slabs, Glyder Fawr, Wales, in 1930 has been awarded an E1 – *plus ça change* . . .

Footless Crow, and Livesey's performance, are said to have stunned the climbing world in 1974. One respected climber reputedly hung up his karabiners and retired after watching Livesey shin up Goat Crag like a gibbon up a flagpole. Said Livesey, 'At the time I was doing routes that were more sustained and bolder than any routes that had been done before. The thing about Footless Crow (so called because even a bird could not find a landing place) is that you have to employ skilful use of runners and ropework to avoid the tremendous amount of rope drag that you get at the top. Footless Crow, like the E3 route Bitter Oasis, is on the Northern Face of Goat Crag, Borrowdale, described in the Fell and Rock Climbing Club guide as 'vegetated, and frequently black and damp. It is also steep, boasts excellent rock, and is continuous to a height of about 250 feet.' The route itself is 'a superb route with an incredible main pitch, which can just be done with two 150 ropes, if used carefully.' The first pitch of about twenty feet shares the route of a climb called Athanor. Livesey says he failed on his first attempt of the main 175 foot pitch of Footless on account of 'inability and fright.' On the second attempt he succeeded. After his initial failure, Livesey had been keen to try again while the problems were fresh in his mind. The only companion he could find on that particular afternooon was a non-climber, a sailor called Robin Witham. Witham held the rope at the foot of the crag while Livesey climbed. Near the top he ran out of rope and finished the final thirty feet of the pitch solo.

'It's a strenuous climb, full of very difficult moves with the weight very much on the hands, very bold, with few nuts for protection.' In place of the standard nut runners that served as belays for the climbing rope, a new form of machined metal chock had been introduced. These are slim wedges or hexagonal sections (nuts) with a wire loop to take a karabiner. The wedges are made in a variety of sizes to slip into the appropriate crack or flake of rock. 'You have to be careful to clip the rope into the runner so the rope doesn't drag or catch over the rock, and of course there's a lot of slack that can be pulling you back. The important thing in ropework is having the strength not just to climb the route but to hang around long enough to select and place your belays, and then have the strength to go on climbing afterwards. It's like a game of chess being two or three moves in advance the whole time, and there's considerable skill involved putting the runners in place.' At one point, Livesey had about seventy feet of rope out on to a couple of dodgy runners. 'This,' said Livesey, 'is what rock climbing's really all about, pushing on when there isn't any protection, and not cracking up and having doubts about your climbing. You cannot give up on it, for once you commit yourself there's no real rest, there are no suitable cracks nor spikes of rock for a runner. The route on the main or crux pitch (the crux is the hardest part of the climb) goes straight for a big overhang.' In addition to the chocks or wedges, they had nylon tape slings, and the relatively new Whillans Harness, designed by Don Whillans, which takes the weight on the thighs, and in the event of a fall makes less of a problem of constriction than the conventional rope around the waist. The protection was prudent but inclined to mar Livesey's performance, not so much technically, but psychologically. 'I always climbed better with no protection, and you had to have control over your mental state, although you'd take a long fall if you came off. I think that characterises most of my climbs, especially the harder ones, for there isn't much protection on them.'

Jill Lawrence, probably the finest woman climber in Britain, who put up many new routes with Livesey as his second, could only remember him taking one proper fall. 'He never used to fall off at all, it was amazing, he was so in control that he could usually climb back down. When Peter started climbing, falling wasn't something you did anyway, because the protection was not sufficiently developed.'

Surely, then, if protection had not advanced much beyond the odd sling belay over a spike of rock (Peascod); the pebbles off the scree as chockstones (Whillans); the nut runners threaded on slings (Bonington and others) – what particular advantage had Livesey, that with the same equipment (or none at all) he could raise the grades from E2 to an astronomic E5? There are several answers to the one question. Firstly, Livesey introduced a very self-disciplined and rigorous training programme which coincided with the new climbing walls that were beginning to appear in sports centres and gymnasiums. Training is by no means new. O.G. Jones trained with weights. Bill Peascod was lifting weights three times a week: 'Training has been in as long as climbing, it's just taken different forms. There used to be an old climber, I think it was A.B. Reynolds, who used to walk around the Lake District with his rucksack full of rocks to train for the Alps. I trained to get strong and hang on cliffs, and I've hung to small holds for up to an hour at a time.' In light contrast to this disciplined approach to training is Don Whillans' attitude, which is typical: 'I start training,' he said firmly, 'when I leave the last pub.'

But Livesey's training was specific and purposeful. 'I realised I'd got the physical potential to climb well, so I set about training for it, practising

Pete Livesey making the first ascent of 'Downhill Racer' on Froggat Edge, Derbyshire in 1976. (PL)

Sheer, exposed and seemingly smooth walls with limited protection are a Livesey speciality, and a particular challenge. Climbing with the assurance of a fly, Livesey tries out a new route in the Sierra Nevada mountains, California in 1977. (PL) climbing on walls. Most climbers, if they train, try and resolve difficult problems – the first ten feet of a difficult piece of rock – which improves their skills and strength, but it doesn't help on long and sustained pitches.' Livesey emphasises this approach with the story of Henry Barber, long the butt of Livesey's brand of waspish humour, who built a replica pitch out of wood in his cellar, 'and trained all winter on it until he could float up it.' A climbing wall is the evening institute version of the outdoor practice of 'bouldering'. Bouldering means exactly what the term implies – you scramble about on boulders, or piles of rock at ground level, as an introduction to climbing or as a means for practising moves. Bouldering helps you to assess your balance and co-ordination of your hands and feet. Climbing walls simulate a rock face: they are brick walls with projections and recesses, slopes and overhangs. 'People now train on climbing walls,' Jill Lawrence explained, 'and they traverse, which builds up stamina and endurance, and lets you know what your body can and can't do. When you try something on a climbing wall, a way of using a hold, and you come across a similar problem on a route, instead of being totally flummoxed and wondering what to do, you think – Aha! I've been in this situation before, and you can figure out what to do.'

Pete Livesey had had ten years' climbing experience before he decided to embark on his assault of contemporary climbing records and ascents, and what could be achieved on various types of rock. 'Gritstone, gives you short but strenuous climbs and "problems". There may be one very difficult move, but once you've done it – that's it! Limestone (the type of rock found near Livesey's home in Malham, Yorkshire) tends to be a little bit steeper, but has more holds on it, and the holds are finger holds rather than hand-jambs (cracks in the rock wide enough to jamb your fist in) or anything like that, and you get long hundred to two hundred foot stretches of overhanging rock, producing a series of fairly hard moves. The volcanic (Lakeland) rock is a bit like limestone, except that there tends to be fewer holds on it, so you have got to keep to natural lines a lot more than you have on limestone. The natural weaknesses are where you find the holds.' Livesey started to train for the limestone and volcanic rocks which offer sustained climbs and the fiercest routes – those that had yet to be conquered. 'So I thought, what's the best way to get good for that kind of thing? The only way you can do sustained climbing is not by going up and down, but by traversing, going along a climbing wall for a hundred feet, then back again. I worked out a training schedule, through a very difficult traverse as hard as I could do. Then I did two of them, then three, until I could manage ten of them with thirty seconds' rest in between. It is very much like athletics interval training, and seems to be the first time that anyone had approached it this scientifically.'

Livesey's remarkable contribution to the sport has to be viewed in its historical context. He was the right person at the right time and introduced the same attitude to climbing that top professional tennis players have towards tennis. Livesey heralded and to some extent personified the long hair and head band activists with their bags of chalk and a hard line in competitiveness. The conservative climbers no doubt saw all this as unethical and were quick to accuse Livesey of cheating during a climb up Gordale Scar. In the climbing world, backbiting and 'taking the piss' (a climbing term) has been elevated to a fine degree of sophistication that merits an E6 6b. Not only had Livesey broken rules, for good measure he had kicked sand in the face of the Yorkshire Mountaineering Club. 'The trouble was that my climbing partner, John Sheard, and myself were not part of the Establishment. Members of the YMC had been trying to free-climb the Face Route on Gordale Scar, and completely unknown to us they had climbed it the week before, but were obliged to use four or five points of aid.' Livesey pre-inspected the route, abseiling down from the top, then made a preliminary top-roped ascent. 'We came along and free-climbed it.' During the climb, Sheard climbed up a rope, removing some pegs that had been used as running belays, but had proved unnecessary. He was spotted doing this and the observer assumed that Livesey and Sheard had rope-climbed part of the ascent. 'The news got back to the Club, who said, "Right, we don't believe any of your routes." They refused to acknowledge them, and because they were part of the establishment it caused us a lot of problems.'

In addition to careful pre-inspection, Livesey thoroughly gardened his climbs on an abseil rope, unlike Whillans who actually gardened as he climbed, showering those below with muck, moss and clumps of grass. Peascod, a decade before Whillans, did not bother with gardening nor pre-inspection. 'I did fifty new climbs in the Lakes, and only remember gardening once. But the way they do it these days, well, I'm just, er, spellbound.' Peascod chuckles with admiration, 'They'll go down and hang on the ropes and tackle the rock with wire brushes until it's pristine in its brightness'.

Perhaps Peascod was unaware that the fashion for landscape gardening had begun in the 1920s. Harry Moss Kelly and his companions cleaned up their climb with a top rope and broom. 'Came to a number of loose blocks',

Kelly wrote in his diary, 'threw those down, did a considerable amount of gardening.'

The advantage of abseiling down while gardening, Livesey claims, is that you can see where all the good holds are, and this is useful if you've got a good memory.

In the late 1960s, before his debut, Livesey practised on some local quarries in Yorkshire, before embarking on a series of hard, limestone ascents, including the episode on Gordale Scar, free-climbing old routes that had previously used points of aid. 'My ambition,' he said, 'was to climb harder than anyone else and pioneer harder routes than anything yet achieved.' Fighting talk. The brash element in Livesey's character and, it must be admitted, his sense of humour at Henry Barber's expense, came with his ascent of Tensor at Tremadog, Gwynedd. It was one of Joe Brown's classic, difficult routes, but Brown had climbed it with three points of aid – three pitons hammered into the rock to gain ascent. Then Henry Barber did a free climb with ropes, so Livesey, ever competitive, went one better and actually soloed the route wearing Hush Puppies. It became a legendary feat. 'I had decided that it was well within my capabilities, and I also did it to take the piss out of Henry Barber.'

In 1972 Livesey went to the Yosemite National Park in California, a centre of American climbing, where the granite cliffs reveal sustained cracks, a type of rock formation that hardly exists in Britain, and which demand a certain type of climbing. You have to imagine a sheer wall of smooth rock, as high as a tower block, with straight vertical cracks running the full length, and about 6" wide. You climb by jamming your hands and feet into the cracks.

On his return home, he tried out his transatlantic style on the unclimbed Wellington Crack at Ilkley Quarry, which yielded to his technique. But if climbing were simply a matter of technique, born of hard training on climbing walls, and experience of a variety of rock types, rock-climbing would be reduced to a free for all, with young and vigorous climbers 'floating up' routes with equal ease. Livesey stressed that technique was only fifty percent of a climber's potential; the remainder was his attitude. 'One of the things a climber must develop is to know how hard a piece of rock he can climb. You can go to a climbing wall and say – I can climb that, but I can't climb that. Now, if it's only a climbing wall it doesn't matter because you are just five feet off the ground anyway. But if you can make the same assessment on rock a hundred feet from the ground, then that's good – it's what I could do. Most climbers can't. Their perception of difficulty changes with height.

They look at a pitch of rock high up and say 'I can't climb that', when in fact they *can* climb it or rather, they could climb it five feet from the ground. So attitude is the ability to know what you can climb in any situation, regardless of protection and height.'

Livesey has a psychological advantage as a result, he believes, of soloing routes early in his carreer, which engendered tremendous self-confidence. Height did not impede his performance, though it does worry a lot of climbers whose technique and potential ability is inhibited by fear. Livesey is able to focus his attention on the problem regardless of the height, and of the protection – or lack of it. In 1974 the time had arrived to demonstrate his virtuosity, so Livesey quit his teaching post at Scunthorpe, and took a year off to devote himself to hard and competitive climbing. The climbing world, particularly in the Lake District, had barely heard of Pete Livesey. He had, as a sort of overture, put up an E2 route called Sally Free and Easy on Pavey Ark in Great Langdale, back in the summer of 1971, and in 1973, with John Sheard, a route called Raindrop, an E1 climb on Black Crag. They should have called it Red Herring, for it was to be followed in 1974 with Footless Crow, Bitter Oasis (E3), Goat Crag (also climbed with Sheard), Nagasaki Grooves on Greatend Crag (E4) and Dry Grasp (E4) on Upper Falcon Crag, the majority climbed free and alone with a back rope.

This system of climbing enables you to climb without having a belayer, or second climber, holding the rope for you. You tie your rope securely to the ground or somewhere near the ground before you start, and you climb by having a series of loops tied in the rope, each loop taking, say, six feet of rope. As you climb you clip each loop into runners. You can work the loops at any interval you like, so if you read the rock before the climb you can judge how often your runners are going to be and where they will be located. The advantage of climbing with a back rope is that you climb alone. Mo Anthoine, climbing consultant on two James Bond films, Safety Officer on the Border Television series, and a designer of climbing equipment, has a broad and impartial view of climbing ethics: 'If someone has found or is about to pioneer a major route, there are lots of people after it, it's that competitive and there are not all that many prime routes left. Climbers try and do a route without anyone watching, but the word gets around, so a climber has to start extra early in the morning – or pretend they are going somewhere else, then sneak back when the coast is clear.'

Once a major route has been pioneered, others attempt to repeat it, but Footless Crow went two years before anyone could do it, and was not repeated again for another five or six years. 'There are,' claims Livesey, 'hundreds of extremely good, skilful rock-climbers who have never done difficult routes. They can do anything you want on boulders, or on climbing walls, but when they try to climb something high up, their potential drops three or four grades because they haven't got this mental capability of concentrating on the task in hand, or displacing the fear of what's to come; their coping techniques are not sufficiently developed. If you are in a frightening situation you've got to force yourself to think about the climb, or to come down.'

Come on down? But what if you are 'committed' and cannot come down? The man in the street – who would much prefer to remain in the street than on the rock – can readily imagine being frozen on the rock for eternity, crucified to a crag with a Lakeland village a thousand feet directly below . . .

Yet climbers insist that the sport is not all that risky. 'Not many people get killed rock-climbing out of the number that do it,' said Livesey encouragingly, 'and though a percentage get injured, it is usually the inexperienced, the beginners.' Chris Bonington said that rock-climbing in the Lake District was probably less dangerous than driving down the M6 Motorway regularly. 'Climbing in the early Fifties had a high level of danger, but statistically the number of fatal accidents has gone down rapidly in the last ten or fifteen years, simply because the actual means of safeguarding yourself has greatly improved.'

The past decade has seen fierce arguments in the pub bars and climbing club huts rooms over the ethics of protection, and in particular the question of the expansion bolt in use since the 1950s. Dedicated purists such as Pete Whillance go around the Lake District climbs, removing the bolts and pitons that climbers have left in. Said Livesey, 'You drill a hole and put a bolt in. This means, in effect, that you are reducing the climb to a five foot boulder problem, so you artificially reduce the danger and that really destroys the essence of climbing.' And that, in a nutshell, is what climbing is all about. It is about risk and danger. Risk rules, and without danger there would be no rock-climbing or mountaineering.

Pete Livesey's last major route in the Lakes was Das Kapital (E5) on Raven Crag, Thirlemere, with Peter Gomersall. He quit while he was at the top and sensibly declined to make a comeback. 'I was quite a competitive climber, and at some stage I found that I was unable physically or technically to climb at the highest grades. In 1981, when there was a new wave in technical grades, and the training wasn't improving my ability, I had to find something else to train at.' Livesey says this matter-of-factly, then laughs, presumably at his inability merely to run with the pack. Athletes are in it to win, but in climbing, as in everything else, the future casts its shadow: 'People are now soloing up routes,' said Livesey thoughtfully, 'that I thought were my hardest climbs.'

Empire has a 40 ft pitch graded 6a for technical difficulty. Women climbers score on the technical aspects of climbing more than on the physical. (AB)

Jill Lawrence and Gill Price. Women have been rock-climbing for well over a hundred years, and in the Alps since the early 19th century. (AB)

6

Jill Lawrence and Gill Price: Empire

'Young fellows,' wrote Lakeland climber C.E. Benson, in 1900, 'especially those who are very strong, will enter a gully, and 'wrestle their way out' by sheer strength and audacity. They arrive at the top, triumphant, but streaming with perspiration and much exhausted. An excellent object lesson for these would be to watch a slight girl climb the same gully with grace and precision, and reach the top with no signs of her exertions save a slightly heightened colour and slightly quickened breathing. It might impress them with a salutary sense of shame, and also with the idea that there is something in climbing to be learnt.'

Benson's comments were not about women as climbers so much as about their style. Women had been climbing for a long time, and were accepted in the climbing world (well, almost) if not by the general public. The feminine influence on rock-climbing actually pre-dated, by sixteen years, Haskett-Smith's ascent of Napes Needle, a feat generally regarded as the birth of rock-climbing, the true beginning of the sport. The occasion was Miss A. Barker's climb to the summit of Pillar Rock in 1870, followed three years later by Mary Westmorland and her two brothers. While men climbers such as O.G. Jones flung themselves at the rock like a puppy leaping on a favourite lap, women climbers were cooler and more calculating. You did not hear about women failing to make the ascent or falling off in groups tied together in the manner of mountain ponies. They were more likely to be like Lucy Walker, who in 1871 was the first woman to climb the Matterhorn. Lucy climbed in a voluminous white linen crinoline, and with her customary nourishment – sponge cake and champagne. But Lucy Walker was by no means the first woman mountaineer, for Henriette d'Angeville had climbed Mont Blanc in 1838 wearing knickerbockers of Scottish tweed lined with red flannel, and she carried with her a blancmange, some prunes

The Ladies Scottish Climbing Club, a year after it was formed in 1908. To qualify for membership demanded the ascent of four 3,000 ft mountains, two rock climbs and two snow climbs. (LSCC)

Emily Kelly, founder of the Pinnacle Club, the rock-climbing club for women. (F & RCC) Emily on Castle Naze. (PC)

Empire, on Raven Crag, is a tough, E3 route. Gill Price fell off near the top, but went on to finish the climb. (BT)

Jill Lawrence, a very determined climber 'with a drive to succeed and fight her way up the hardest routes'. (BT)

and a carrier pigeon. The pigeon, bearing a message of her success, was released from the summit, but alas, it was the season of *la chasse* and a farmer shot it down.

The women mountaineers came, of course, from the same social background as the men, and in most cases their social standing was as high as the peaks to which they aspired. A typical and most illustrious example was the heiress Elizabeth Hawkins-Whitshed. At the age of eighteen she married Colonel Fred Burnaby, whose splendid portrait by Tissot is in the National Portrait Gallery, London, a six-foot-four officer of the Blues, and reputedly the strongest man in the army. Although Lizzie suffered a lung disorder – or perhaps because of it – she skated, skiied and became a redoubtable mountaineer, making the first winter ascent of the Aiguille du Tour, the Col du Tacul and Col du Chardonnet. Twice widowed, she finally married Aubrey Le Blond, and it was as Lizzie Le Blond that she enjoyed most of her fame as a mountaineer, climbing, as was her custom, accompanied by a lady's maid, and wearing climbing breeches under her skirt. She founded the Ladies' Alpine Club in 1907 and was its first President. 'The debt that women climbers of all generations still owe her,' wrote Cicely Williams, 'is incalculable'.

The following year, the women climbers north of the border formed the Ladies' Scottish Climbing Club. Its founders were Mrs Jane and Miss Mabel Inglis Clark and Lucy Smith, the first Treasurer.

There were many outstanding Victorian women climbers: Kathleen Richardson, in the 1880s, made 116 alpine ascents, six being first ascents, and fourteen were firsts by a woman. She made a first woman's ascent of the Meije – the mountain had been climbed a decade earlier by Castelnau and Gaspard – in one day, and the climb included a pitch that almost defeated W.A.B. Coolidge who wrote: 'the descent of this wall will always remain in my mind as the most arduous and terrible piece of climbing it has ever fallen my lot to perform.' While Katy Richardson was pioneering in the Alps, a Miss Koecher climbed to the top of Napes Needle, and was there photographed by her companion Professor Dixon. A large print appeared in a shop window in the Strand, in 1891, and it was this picture that inspired O.G. Jones to rush off to Wasdale and climb the Needle himself.

The climbing world was, of course, dominated by men but, as every woman will appreciate, while the men drew at their cigars (climbers have always been dedicated smokers) and regaled each other with fantastic tales of unbelievable male heroism, and while O.G. Jones traversed the Wasdale

Inn billiard room in his socks, the ladies just got on with it. During Ladies' Week at Wasdale, for example, Annie and Evelyn Seatree climbed Moss Ghyll, North Climb of Pillar Rock, Scafell Pinnacle by Steep Ghyll and Slingsby's Chimney, Kern Knotts Chimney, Oblique Chimney, Doctor's Chimney, Pillar Rock by Right and Left Jordan, and Pisagh Direct, all in ten days. In 1912 the last three and most difficult pitches on the North-East Climb of Pillar Rock were climbed by a party which included a Miss Capper. Although the Fell and Rock Club admitted members of both sexes, women climbers wanted to run their own show. They wanted a club which would mark their growing interest in rock-climbing, as the ladies' Alpine Club had marked for women their success as mountaineers.

The woman who took the initiative was Emily Kelly, wife of the pioneer Lakeland climber (though a Mancunian) Harry Moss Kelly. It was to be called the Pinnacle Club, and one of its principal aims was to encourage independence and self-confidence. Emily Kelly thought that women were inclined to take a subordinate role in climbing and reduced their climbing potential by allowing men to direct them. 'As in other walks of life,' she wrote, 'women wanted to find their own feet. It was splendid for some women to be always able to borrow crutches in the shape of a man's help, and a man's rope, but it is even better to find that we have feet of our own, and can climb some things as well as a man climber.'

The Pinnacle Club was founded in 1921, and if Emily's intention had been to spark off a new wave of endeavour she certainly succeeded, and it would be a fitting tribute to her memory, for she died in 1922 in a climbing accident. A friend of the Kellys', Blanche Eden-Smith, seconded Kelly on his greatest climb, the first ascent of Moss Ghyll Grooves, in 1926, and in 1931 she climbed The Plaque Route and The Central Route on Bowfell Buttress, also with Kelly.

It was a woman climber who first drew attention to the possibilities offered by Harrison's Rocks – Nea Morin. Emancipation on the rock face was well and truly established in 1929 when Nancy Ridyard made six first ascents by a woman on Dow Crag, and several more on Gimmer. The Gimmer Crag routes had been pioneered by George Bower and Arthur Wakefield, and most were rated VS or Severe. Between them, Bower and Wakefield effectively wrapped up all the climbs on what was called the 'Gentlemen's Side' of Gimmer (as opposed to the tourists' routes), including such routes as Hiatus, The Crack, Asterisk and Joas; in all, six severe climbs. Then along came Nancy Ridyard with her guide book and methodically climbed everything Bower and Wakefield had climbed and just to rub it in teamed up with J.A. Musgrave and put up Musgrave's Traverse, a Severe route.

The mountaineering world, and rock-climbing circles, did not seem especially intolerant of feminine autonomy, but of course they were all more or less of the same social class and they doubtless all knew each other. There were plenty of women who accompanied their climbing husbands to the Lakes but declined to hang on ropes, preferring to walk the fells. However, for the novelist and climber Freya Stark 'climbing was the key of a world a little above the human world and beyond it, where one could always find a refuge from friction and time.'

The competitiveness and the expression of intense physical energy that some men climbers eventually find enervating seems largely absent among women climbers. Women's motives for climbing are rather more abstract and less obvious than men's, although all climbers enjoy the rewards of mastering a difficult climb. Gill Price, who with her partner Jill Lawrence are perhaps the most successful women's climbing team in Britain, does not regard the sport as emphatically physical, nor especially competitive. 'We don't really compete with men. There's a lot of healthy competition among women climbers, but perhaps it is more in the sense of achievement than competition. I think that to some extent because standards are rising quite rapidly, women are aware that there is now a possibility of closing the gap between what women consider is possible, and what men are doing. You begin to realise that by accepting a separate standard and thinking, "Oh, well, I'm climbing well enough for a woman", you are losing opportunities. I think that women have a better chance of closing the gap on the technical side of climbing rather than the physical – but when you get to the harder climbs there are only a limited number of holds, so you can do it or you can't, regardless of your sex.'

In Britain the women currently able to do hard climbs in the higher grades number a mere thirty or so. 'Women climbers keep in touch with each other,' said Jill Lawrence, 'Britain's a small enough place to be able to do that.'

The two women, Jill Lawrence and Gill Price, seem well matched as a team. Jill Lawrence, the taller of the two, is the outwardly more forceful. She has an open, frank appeal, a fair curly mop of hair and wears large round bifocal glasses. The abrasive edge of her personality is less keen, and she has mellowed, according to those who know her well. She was born in Chester in 1951, one of a large family. Gill Price was born in Colwyn Bay, Wales, in 1953, the younger of two girls. Lawrence and Price met at

Gill Price following up first pitch of 'Empire'. (CB)

Bingley College, Yorkshire, where Jill Lawrence was already an experienced climber. She plucked Gill Price out of the chorus line, so to speak, while the latter was practising on a climbing wall. 'She's got a very strong personality,' said Gill Price, 'and on the surface can seem very aggressive, a lot of which she channels into rock climbing. As a climber she is very pushy. I've seen her struggling and shaking her way up a route, and there's no way that she would fail to do it. She is a very determined woman, with a drive to succeed and fight her way up the hardest routes. She must be one of the best climbers there is because she has the will to achieve and keep up a very high standard.'

Peter Livesey reckons that Jill Lawrence is probably the best woman climber in Britain, and he should know, since they were partners together and, with John Sheard, pioneered some of Livesey's hard routes. 'Our partnership eventually broke up because of restlessness on my part. It was on two levels, a climbing partnership and a personal relationship. During our time together my standards improved tremendously and I learned a lot from Peter.' Her own personal ambition as a climber gradually came to conflict with Livesey's. She seconded his climbs, but wanted to lead routes of her own. 'There was a big difference in what I could lead and what I could second – a full two grades. I decided that I should do more leading, but it meant that I had to drop my standard, climbing routes that were easier, but at least I could lead them. Over the past few years I have been trying to close the gap between what I could second for Peter and what I can lead myself.'

The relationship reached a pitch that, in climbing terms, might be rated E6, 6c. 'I was very restless and didn't know what I wanted, and I began to do very destructive things.' Through Livesey, Jill Lawrence had made a name for herself as a climber, and now wanted complete autonomy, so Livesey abseiled out of the partnership and they went their separate ways. If Jill Lawrence had lived at the same time as Lucy Walker, it is hard to say which one might have been the first to climb the Matterhorn, though Lucy by contrast had a quiet, unassuming disposition, more like Gill Price. 'A really quiet person when you first meet her,' says Jill Lawrence, 'she tends to stay in the background and it takes a fair time to get to know her.' Small and slightly built with dark, shoulder-length hair, Gill Price is an excellent climber and was one of the team to complete the remaining pitches on the eliminate climb Breaking Point, an E2 on Gimmer Crag, with Livesey, John Sheard and Jill Lawrence. An eliminate climb, by the way, is the most direct possible route and allows no wandering or variations in its course.

Both girls are teachers, and the partnership faltered for a while when Jill Lawrence went to work in America, but they recently resumed the climbing partnership and tackled the E3 route Empire, on Raven Crag, for the Border Television cameras. 'Jill and I have been friends for a long time, we spend quite a bit of time together socially, but when it comes to climbing you get in tune and can, to a certain extent, predict things – I can see when she's worried about something, and vice-versa.' It is a cliché, of course, but women do seem to possess an intuitive knack in assessing a partner's moods or thoughts – sometimes in advance. Disconcerting perhaps, but probably valuable when climbing together and providing a foundation of co-operation that a male partnership might well lack. Both girls are able to lead through routes, which means they take it in turns, since both can climb equally hard and to about the same standard. Physique is obviously very important, and it is this that contributes to the feminine style of climbing that C.E. Benson mentioned. As Jill Lawrence explained: 'When you first start climbing you haven't got upper body strength, so you tend to be much better on your feet. If you get the right weight and balance you can then rest your arms a lot. Even when climbs are steep you can often get your feet on, and you are rarely in those situations where you have to do pull-ups, so women tend to look a little more graceful.' Benson observed that women made good climbers. 'They have a good sense of balance, less weight than men and all their strength is in the right place. It is in arm strength that they are weakest.'

The mountaineer Cicely Williams, making the inevitable comparison between men and women climbers, said that 'men are, on the whole, better climbers than women and they have greater reserves of strength – although women are capable of greater endurance.'

'It's a sport,' said Jill Lawrence firmly, 'where most of the participants are men, and there are dominant values in it – male values, and women have to decide whether or not to accept this – you know, what's considered an achievement and what isn't.' As Chris Bonington wrote about his wife, Wendy, 'If she had wanted to take up climbing, she could probably not have followed me up the routes that I wanted to lead, and even if she could, I would not have been certain that she had the strength to hold me if I fell off.' Wendy Bonington's climbing debut was brief and final.

'This is only a Diff,' I assured her.

'What's a Diff?' she asked, bemused.

'Difficult.'

'Couldn't we do something easy to start with?'

'Difficult is easy – I know it sounds contradictory, but beyond Diff there are four more grades – anything easier than this would be a walk. You won't have any trouble on this and we'll soon have you doing VSs.' As it turned out, Wendy didn't display a natural aptitude for rock-climbing.

'You·can get a man partner who will encourage you to lead,' said Gill Price, but I think they are a bit rare. What can sometimes happen is that you can be offered to lead a pitch, but as soon as it looks as though you might want to back off it, they jump at the chance to lead, rather than give you the encouragement you need to climb up it.' Young male climbers, desperate to succeed, are prey to impatience and lack of experience in their relationships with women climbers. 'There's always been a sort of role for women,' Gill Price continued with a trace of asperity, 'and that's to hold the rope and take·the gear out. But on the rock, the men just want to rush in and take over as soon as they see you might be failing.' There is, in all this, an unfortunate overtone of primitive tribal mores where, says Jill Lawrence, 'there are thousands of male climbers around, all supporting each other and pushing each other to do things, and it's very acceptable for them to do this, but it is much harder for women climbers to band together in a supportive group.'

The cynical view is that men do not want to encourage women climbers, because rock-climbing is traditionally a male preserve, inevitably involved with masculine competitiveness; women are accepted in the climbing world so long as they remain a separate entity.

Jill Lawrence thinks that women have the potential to climb as well as the best men climbers, 'if you consider that in climbing you are just dealing with a weight to strength ratio. Most women have a smaller frame and therefore don't have as much weight to haul up. But by training you can develop strength and endurance to improve this power to weight ratio. Woman *can* climb as hard as men, but only women with a light frame where you've got slim hips and broad shoulders, and where training can build upper body strength.'

There would probably be far more women climbers if there was more organised instruction at leisure centres and on climbing walls; it is not seen, right now, as a sport or a pastime for women although there is no reason that this should be so. During the winter, both Jill and Gill spend most of their spare time training on climbing walls though, as they admit, it can get boring, but it does produce results. The most interesting thing, though, is the risk factor. Jill Lawrence points out that men are encouraged from birth to take risks, or at least to accept the fact that risk is part of their

114

Jill Lawrence, Gill Price and Chris Bonington on the scree below Raven Crag. 'When you get to the harder climbs', said Gill Price, 'there are only a limited number of holds, so you can do it or you can't, regardless of your sex.' (BT)

future; 'girls are generally channelled away from risk from an early age, so that women start off with a disadvantage, and are also discouraged from physical action.'

Both sexes, however, enjoy and benefit from a degree of risk. 'Risk is a really important part of climbing,' said Jill Lawrence, 'but the skilful climber tries to minimise the risk. There's no death wish involved – all you are trying to do is get to the top safely.'

In climbing, risks are usually calculated, and everything is weighed very carefully before you make a decision. If you are sufficiently skilful and confident, then it's really like deciding that, if you are driving a car, you can get round a bend at high speed. Jill Lawrence confesses that she often gets scared and has to struggle with herself to decide whether or not the risk is acceptable. Women do not, as a rule, go deliberately into a risky situation. It could be argued that women are less willing to gamble with their lives than men. On the whole they are less likely to push themselves physically to the limits than men and this makes women's attitude to climbing fundamentally different from men's. On the other hand, women enjoy the 'buzz' that is the reward from a successful climb as much as men: 'Whatever level you are climbing at', says Gill Price, 'regardless of your sex, there is a great sense of achievement after a big effort, when you manage to get up a rock climb. I've been leading routes for the past five years, and it is always the same – you get this tremendous sensation having got to the top. You get a tremendous buzz, an adrenalin rush, especially when you have put yourself in risky or very technical situations that you then manage to get through and triumph over. You can get quite frightened on a route, and at the end you are just really glad that you've got it over with. Yet, the very next day you will put yourself in an almost identical situation – it's just that you get hooked on it.'

For the courageous, resilient and restless mountaineer and rock-climber Gwen Moffat, who in 1953 became the first woman to acquire a professional guide's certificate, there is 'a mental and physical relaxation, a loosening of the muscles so complete that even the face relaxes and the eyes widen and one's body becomes light and supple – a pliable and co-ordinated entity – when one is shown a climb as a horse is shown a jump. In that exquisite moment before a hard move, when one looks and understands, there may lie an answer to the question why one climbs. You are doing something hard, so hard that failure could mean death, but because of the knowledge and experience you are doing it safely. This safety depends on yourself; there is no other factor: no horse or piece of machinery to let you down. What you accomplish is by your own efforts, and the measure of your success is the width of your margin of safety.'

Non-climbers, those millions of feet-on-the-ground people who regard climbing with awe and respect, but in comprehension probably think of a climb as going up a rock face that is virgin territory, untouched by human hand or foot. The truth is, of course, that most crags are as well-trodden as the steps leading up to Montmartre. You are aware, on a climb, of those who have been before you. The holds are worn and shiny-smooth – they may even have rubber and chalk on them. Prehistoric, rusty pitons and expansion bolts and bongs ('bongs' are pieces of perforated girder, like an RSJ, to be stuffed into large cracks for a belay, or to support the crag) may be encountered *en route*. But there is a certain solace in knowing that if others have done it – so can you.

Jill Lawrence and Gill Price recently climbed the Empire route together on Raven Crag in Thirlemere. To get to the crag, you leave the lakeside road and climb steeply through larch and pine woods until, at the top of the in-cline the path is joined by another to make a broader ascent to the foot of the scree. Now you have to seek the most convenient route across the dove-grey and lichen-green boulders, through which an occasional shrub or bush thrusts itself. It is difficult, unless you are used to pick your way over the tumbled boulders, and it requires balance and caution; the stones are unstable and roll downwards with a sudden clatter as you scramble for a footing. At last at the top of the slope the scree thins out and gives way to fern, bracken, hardy grass and firmer volcanic rock. A ragged dirt path winds steeply towards the base of the crag – but the ravens that gave the crag its name are not much in evidence – only a helicopter and a passing jet plane. From here you can survey the wall of rock – a huge scooped-out portion to the left, the Cave, as though someone had come along with an outsize ice-cream scoop and removed part of the rock. The lower face of the rock is hospitable to ferns, bell heather, stonecrop, storksbill and toadflax. Higher up though, where the climbers must go, the rock is barren.

To Gill Price the crag is 'a lovely piece of rock with a very long second pitch – it's the crux pitch of the route because there's a hard technical move about a third of the way up, and Jill Lawrence climbed it very well. But even the first pitch is no doddle. I'd talked to somebody who said that the technical grade was about 5b and I knew that I could cope with that, although from below it looked as though I couldn't get any runners in at all. As I started the climb I found a place for a small wire, and you could see the places where people had been putting their hands and feet. There was even some chalk on the handholds, but the footholds had been rubbed clean. Some of the rock had lichen on it, but where people had placed their feet the rock was clean, so it was pretty obvious to know what to do.' Jill Lawrence paused, as all rock climbers must, to regain their equilibrium and sense of proportion. 'I felt really sure of myself and I just felt that there was no way I was going to fall off this, it just didn't enter my head. I felt that I was achieving a very smooth rhythm where you feel as though you float up the rock with no effort whatsoever. There's no real working it out as it were, or at least you are not conscious of it. It is instantaneous, working out the moves, as long as there's no hesitation you just flow over them, and the next hold appears and you just move up for that, and it's right, and then the next one, and the next, and it becomes self-fulfilling, and then you get a whole string of easy-flowing moves coming together and then suddenly you think ... Oh, maybe I'll put a runner in here, so you start to look around and there isn't anywhere for a runner, but it doesn't matter. You just keep going because you feel so good about the way you are moving over the rock, and that's how I felt on the groove, and in fact there was a place higher up where I could stop and I was able to put a runner in, and higher up still there was a good ledge and there was an old peg (piton) stuck in a crack. Mind you, it was stuck out two or three inches, but by tying it off near its base, that made it a pretty safe, secure runner.'

Why is it that ironmongery gets left in crags? Well, when a climber leads, he or she puts the protection into the cracks, or flakes of rock on the ascent. Piton, bolts, chocks, slings over spikes, or whatever, are placed *en route* to the top. At the head of each pitch or stance, the leader belays his second, who follows up the route, removing each belay as he climbs – he 'cleans up the route'. If the leader has hammered a piton in too firmly, and the second cannot remove it. the ironmongery gets left in the crag. Some pitons have been left in as points of aid to assist future climbers up 'impossible' pitches. This has particularly incensed Don Whillans: 'I was told that one climb I did in the Lake District had two spikes (pitons) put in it, but I didn't put them in, it was the bloke that was trying to do this before me was putting them in, and I used them, and finished the climb – and nobody has been able to do that climb without them two spikes, even the 5a or 6b or whatever the hell it is, but the guide book has excluded the climb altogether now, because they felt the spikes spoiled the crag. *So they've just wiped out this climb that's been in the guide books for twenty bloody years!* The spikes are still there, I believe, according to the lads who climb in the Lakes, but the

118

fellow that wrote the bloody book, he's wiped out history! Now even he's given up climbing!'

The top pitch of Empire has now been reached by Jill Lawrence: 'The top pitch was harder, the crux of the climb, steeper rock, a small bulge that you had to pull over, there was a peg for protection there but it had been in some time, and they'd begun to corrode.' (Maybe they were Whillans' pegs?) As for Gill Price: 'You make this really gymnastic move on the small finger holds – and I thought it would be all over once I passed the peg, and then you're stood there teetering about, just above this little roof, trying to work out the next move. It's just a thin little move, but you have to be bold because you're leaving the peg behind – and that's your protection. I think I actually talk to myself. I think I may have been saying "calm down" or something when I did it, because I was leaving this peg, and felt a bit frightened. Then it was just one move and afterwards steady climbing to the top. But it was a very good route. A nice route.'

The essence of climbing is that it is a calculated risk. 'You are,' as Jill Lawrence said, 'testing yourself, and putting yourself out on a limb. And although you are climbing with another person, you really are totally responsible for your own actions, and you just accept that, and there are very few situations I think in our society where you can actually do that.' The sport must make the climber endlessly self-critical, since he or she is under constant test, and every few feet of rock is graded like an examination paper. But climbing also offers a great deal of pleasure and self satisfaction. For Gill Price, as for hundreds of climbers, 'it's an exciting sport. A sport that has taken me to lots of places, in America and in Europe. And I can't think of anything else that I would do that would enable me to travel, meet lots of new people, and have really wonderful holidays. I can't think of any other physical sport that would do that and that gives you a lot of excitement and a big buzz at the end of the day.'

7

Pete Whillance: Incantations

Pete Whillance is arguably the boldest and the most audacious of the climbers discussed in this book – or probably anywhere else for that matter. We know that Peter Livesey was an intrepid climber, but he was calculating, methodical, and he knew exactly how far he could go and exactly what he could do. There is a possibility that Pete Whillance may be mad – though you could suspect that of any of the climbers in this book – but he does not seem mad. Indeed, Whillance is relaxed, pleasant, affable, cool, very articulate and also very knowledgeable about climbing history and techniques. But he has, in his own words, 'pushed the boat out somewhat' having taken considerable risks and having suffered some extreme falls.

The titles of some of his routes reveal his preoccupation with danger: Take it to the Limit, Edge of Extinction; Post Mortem; Supernatural; Risk Business. It is a risk business if you do take it to the limit – Whillance has taken many climbs to the limit, and well beyond. He may be the last of the Lakeland climbers ever to practise this bold, almost flamboyant style of climbing. The systems and techniques of protection have advanced to a point where climbers can fall off with impunity; they will fall five feet, or six feet, and then try again. They will not fall, as Whillance has done, fifty feet, a hundred feet, a hundred and fifty feet like a free-fall parachutist who forgets to pull the cord. As Pete Whillance says, he is 'getting a bit over the hill,' or as his near-namesake Don Whillans put it, 'He's unusual in the way that he is a lot older than most of the young top rock climbers. He's thirty-six and that's ancient, oh, aye. Yet he's doing a lot of very hard routes, and right with it.' Pete Whillance was born in Urmston in 1948, and like Livesey was the eldest of three children. He was educated at a local grammar school, then took a chemistry course at a Manchester college. He studied for two years until he discovered that he was not a chemist but a climber – climbing intruded into his work and his future plans, as it did into Chris Bonington's brief career with Unilever.

Whillance's début as a climber came when two fellow students, expert climbers, invited him out for a day's climbing to Castle Naze, a gritstone outcrop in Derbyshire. It was like introducing Nicki Lauda to bumper cars. They ambled up a Moderate grade climb and down again, Whillance polite but bored, until they said, 'What would you really like to do?' Pete Whillance pointed out a climb graded, unknown to him, as a VS. His companions started to explain the system of protection and ropework, but Whillance just went straight up the rock, solo. Then as an encore soloed a second VS, and realised he'd found his vocation. That's what climbing is – not a sport but a vocation!

So Whillance began climbing at the age of seventeen, and proved himself to be a natural. His long-time climbing partner, Dave Armstrong, with whom Whillance did the Border Television climb, Incantations, says that he is cool, calculating and very competitive, and likes to keep on top. Competitiveness seems to run like Ariadne's thread through the labyrinths of the climber's psyche. Lakeland climber Peter Botterill, a close friend of Whillance's, says 'all climbers are competitive, and they are lying if they tell you otherwise.'

Once seriously involved in the climbing world, one becomes involved in the overall pattern of achievement. 'Everyone watches a new climb,' said Whillance resignedly, 'and they are waiting to see if you can do it, and you can't climb in secret anymore. There are a lot more climbers now than there used to be, and the grapevine is very extensive. There are three national magazines on climbing, and all the latest information is being published on what's being done and who's doing it. Information is freely available, and everybody reads the magazines – you *have* to. There's a sort of hierarchy – climbers who are working their way up through the grades getting better and better. Then you get the climbers at the top of the grades, who then start doing new routes in a particular area. Then you arrive at the stage where one or two climbers are accepted as the Godfathers of an area – the Lake District, Wales, Peak District, Pembrokeshire, and so on. Climbers then start to dominate other areas by going and doing the hardest climbs there, and also putting up new routes, until there are one or two doing the hardest climbs in Britain. Now it has even got beyond that. There are world rank climbers, all moving around the world doing the hardest climbs. So it *is* competitive, but not directly as one athlete competing against another.'

Pete Whillance, one of Lakeland's boldest climbers, and a leader of the free-climbing activists of the past decade. (CB)

Great Gable, Wasdale. (ICL)

Climbers desire to see their sport, their vocation, their obsession as above competitiveness. And this, perhaps, stems from its root as a sport for gentlemen, who prefer to lose honourably rather than to win dishonourably. 'I look at the sport of rock climbing as any other sport, whether it's football, cricket, golf or whatever one is doing. You are trying to improve your skill and ability – but with climbing you back that skill against your life; if you are not up to it you may well hurt yourself. It's just another sort of challenge added to the main theme of testing your ability. Even if I kill myself, I can look at it quite clearly and say that, subjectively, it will be my fault and I will have made an error of judgement.'

Whillance made a spectacular error of judgement on a route called Top Gear on Raven Crag and, as he confessed, it was bravado born of competitiveness that made him incautious. 'There was another team there that was attempting the route, had failed, and offered me a chance at it, and I took it on although it was raining; normally I wouldn't attempt it in the rain. Also, I hadn't inspected the route beforehand – I would always abseil down and look at it.' Pete Botterill said that Whillance had got to within a few feet of the crag top. He was on a sloping ramp that was covered in green slime and there was nothing to hold on to. 'Pete came off and fell 120 feet, ripping out all his protection as he went down, breaking two karabiners.' Whillance hit the scree at the foot of the crag. 'My head just hit the ground on the extension of the rope.' Climbing rope stretches; if rope didn't stretch it would be much more likely to break, but the stretch uses up kinetic energy, so you have a greater chance of surviving. Whillance survived – just. 'I was fortunate that I only bashed the top of my head and face,' said Whillance casually, 'due to the extension of the rope, which returned to its normal length and I ended up fifteen feet from the ground.' In other words, Whillance came down like a yo-yo. 'He detached himself from the rope, and drove off to hospital,' said Botterill. 'Then he went back later and made the first ascent.'

Whillance was certainly the most influential Lakeland climber from the mid-1970s to the early 1980s. 'I started doing new routes in the Lake District in 1974, like Brutus on Buckstone How (E3) and Eclipse on Pavey Ark (E4), and continued for a ten-year period averaging thirty to forty new routes a year. In terms of quantity that's a vast amount more than anyone else has done, and in terms of difficulty a lot of the climbs are of the top nature E4 and E5 and hopefully a lot of them are very good.'

When Peter Livesey left the Lake District following his virtuoso performance of 1974, he returned by public demand to make a few encores, such as Scrutineer, Tristar, Breaking Point, Eastern Hammer, Peels of Laughter, and finally Das Kapital in 1978. The local climbers were still demoralised by the shock of seeing Footless Crow conquered by Livesey which, in terms of rock-climbing, was rather like watching someone soloing the Eiger in pyjamas. Whillance stepped forward to rally the broken clans. 'It took the locals, myself included, a year or two to get to Livesey's standard, and it was probably 1976-7 before we were producing climbs at his level, and a year after that before we could produce routes that were harder than those he put up.' Two such climbs were Whillance's Desperado, and Take it to the Limit. Whillance was a very suitable candidate to succeed Livesey since he had learned Livesey's technique and powered it with his own brand of daredevil tactics.

'A lot of the climbs I put up are very, very serious. Serious to the extent that you may kill yourself if you fall off. In 1978 I did Take it to the Limit, and at E6 the climb was a grade harder than anything that had been done at the time. Technically it was 6b, a level that had already been achieved, but for seriousness it was way ahead.' Technical gradings are in numerical progression and supplement the E gradings for seriousness, so that a climb rated E6 6b means that there is a high element of risk involved, and that it is technically difficult requiring some hard moves. The secondary grading, from 5a to 6b or 6c may also be applied to individual pitches. Take it to the Limit is a route on Deer Bield crag, with a fearsome 100 foot 6b pitch, and just Whillance's cup of tea. He and Dave Armstrong, his second on the climb, were watched by Ron Fawcett who, with Gerry Moffat, are reckoned to be the two finest climbers of the moment.

'It was very fortunate in many respects that Fawcett watched us do it, and he did the second ascent immediately after us, while the chalk was still on, and we sort of coached him up it and told him where to place the one or two runners that were necessary – but it hasn't been repeated since that day.'

At the moment there are a few climbs tentatively graded E7, but when a new grade is suggested it takes a while before it can be *established* and agreed upon – there has to be a concensus of opinion among the top climbers that one stage has been reached and a new grade is in evidence. 'You'll find a lot of argument about whether or not you can clearly define new grades, but E6 has been *established* a long time now.' One problem is that grading tends to cover a wide spectrum of difficulty even within the same grade. 'A climb that we might grade E5 6b, is a far, far different proposition to Footless Crow. That was *established* as the first of its grade,

125

'*Protection*' is the climber's security against a fall. The rope is 'belayed' to the rock, passing through metal 'karabiners'. These are linked to 'chocks' – metal wedges jammed in cracks in the rock. Should the climber fall, this system of 'running belays' (runners) checks his descent. (CB)

'A lot of the climbs I put up are very, very serious. Serious to the extent that you may kill yourself if you fall off.' Whillance on Great Gable. (CB)

but it is absolute rock-bottom (no pun intended) in that grade, and if done today Footless Crow would barely make E4 6b.' This is not to denigrate Livesey's achievement, it is simply that technical advances have eliminated the original difficulties. Climbers have now arrived in the era of advanced protection, of chalky fingers and friends in high places, of very fine belays and – dare one mention it – expansion bolts. Chalk, magnesium carbonate or gymnastic chalk, was introduced from America in about 1975. 'It is universally accepted now, and it is really essential. Chalk absorbs perspiration and keeps your fingers dry,' but it has its critics who object to the rock face appearing as though it had been liberally dusted for fingerprints.

A 'friend' is a cam device on a spring. You pull the trigger and it collapses so that you can insert it in a crack, when the cams expand to fill the crack. They even work on upside-down flakes of rock and in flared cracks. Friends were first designed in 1974, but did not appear until the late 1970s – one of their greatest advantages is that you can operate them much faster than using a metal chock belay. In addition to friends are the new micro nuts on very fine, high-tensile wire, for use in very thin cracks. These came in during the past few years and have allowed climbers to belay with greater frequency, often putting the nuts in clusters, since they do have a tendency to burst out of the rock under the full body weight of a falling climber.

To the climber's modern armoury you can add footwear. PAs were the climber's shoe, and a lot of people still prefer them to modern footwear which uses rubber technology to provide the highest possible adhesion. 'The latest thing is sticky boots, where the rubber is actually sticky and you can smear it with your feet. If there is a tiny ripple on the rock face you just put your foot above it, and you *smear* your foot down so it sticks to the rock.' So now the crags are not only covered with chalk, but with rubber as well – rather like a repaired puncture on a tyre.

Then there is the sticht plate. The second climber, who is belaying the leader, wears this on his harness, the rope passing through the device which locks the rope in the event of a fall. The conventional belaying technique, as Chris Bonington explained, works like this: 'You just passed the rope around your waist and wrapped it around one wrist. If the leader had a thirty foot fall on just one runner you'd have a violent pull upwards if the runner held, on a thirty foot fall it could break, and if you were a tiny bit dozy and let the rope slide you could burn your hands quite badly. If you use a sticht plate the rope is locked on straight away.' The plate provides an extra safety measure and is 'idiot proof' and gives strong psychological security to the leader. As Whillance pointed out, 'I have taken bad falls from routes that are technically hard, but not all that serious, and they don't count because that is now standard practice in climbing. All hard climbs are the same, and climbers will fall off all day – just a short fall, two, three, four, five days in a run, just falling continuously off a route, trying to get up it, but knowing the protection is there, and that they won't come to much harm. That doesn't count really – everybody does that.'

As for expansion bolts, these are a subject of some controversy, as you have to drill a hole and thus scar the rock in order to insert the bolt. It is not used as a point of aid, only as a belay. But, as Whillance says, 'The guy in the street thinks that a climber just bangs things into the rock to swing up on them – 'Oh, you just bang these pitons in and climb on them.' Climbers have been fighting for years to get over to people that we are *free climbers*. Just because in the late 1960s there was a band of climbers who did use a lot of aid, we've been stuck with the label ever since.'

There is a hard core in Pete Whillance though it is not immediately evident. It only becomes obvious when you study his climbs. He is ambitious as far as climbs go, and he is a perfectionist – 'tries to do well at everything,' says Botterill. He seems to be able to make his body do what his mind orders even if it is impossible. Well, would *you* propel yourself up a sheer wall, two hundred feet high, with a surface the texture of freshly baked bread, with a length of rope and a few pieces of wire?

'You tend to find that there are many good technical climbers, who can reach the highest levels, but they can only do it when they know they are safe, when protection is available, and it's just a game.' This, of course, is the Livesey creed. 'When you put those same people in the position where if they try and do those moves they might fall off and get killed – then it is a totally different game; there are very few climbers who are prepared to commit themselves to the point where they put their lives at risk. You tend to think of it as the difference between soloing and leading climbs. If you take anybody out soloing routes, they will refuse to go on climbs that are anywhere near their limit of their ability. They will solo at two grades easier than they could top rope. Your brain will not allow you to get that close to your actual level of ability, where you might overstretch yourself. The ability to climb at the very edge of your limit and remain cool is something else entirely. It needs a lot of mental control to prevent the brain starting to wander. Nervousness makes you lose energy and everything goes to pieces. Once that happens you are going to fall off.'

With Whillance, falling off is usually a calculated risk. 'I fell off Hodge Close last year and went sixty feet to the ground. Other people had been looking at this climb and decided against it because the rock was so poor. I knew that there was a fair chance the holds would break, but I decided to have a go against my better judgement. In this case three holds went on me in quick succession.' Whillance chuckled at the recollection – 'there was no way out except down. I cracked a couple of ribs I think.'

The crag, the cliff, the mountain provide the climber with the raw material against which he pits his strength and works out his destiny, whether it is getting to the top or falling off – some you win, some you lose. 'I always think that the rock has to have a fighting chance,' said Whillance earnestly. 'Nowadays there are very few people producing serious climbs, there's an attitude that they'll abseil down and put pegs and bolts in, and bring the climb down to their level – not from a point of view of aid, but of seriousness. I'm against that. If you go and look at a piece of rock, that rock offers you a challenge, physically you have to decide whether you are capable of doing it, and also the level of protection. If natural protection isn't available in the cracks and you are not prepared to go solo without that protection, then the rock has beaten you, and you should leave it to another generation of climbers. The rock has beaten you as much psychologically by not providing the protection as it has physically in not providing the holds. And so these serious climbs challenge you to do them without protection, and I've taken some screaming falls at times because of this philosophy.'

Usually, after taking a 'screaming fall' Whillance climbs back up again. He fell sixty feet off a route called Midsummer Night's Dream (E5) – why not Midsummer Night's Scream? Like the living yo-yo that he is, Pete Whillance plummeted down attached to the rope, hit a ledge with his feet, and the elastic tension on the rope bounced him into the air where he hit his head on an overhang. Unfortunately he had his tongue out at the time ... Whillance part-severed his tongue and cut two fingers badly. He went back up the route, fell again, but finally made it to the top. All in a day's climbing. But then Whillance is one of the 'activists' like Jeff Lamb, Dave Armstrong, Ed Cleasby, Ron Matheson and Ricki Graham: all fatalists producing routes with names like Coma, Jaws, Autopsy and Verdict.

And now, even these 'tigers' – which the term 'activist' replaces – have been surpassed by the new wave, not a few of whom prefer to be unemployed and on the dole so that they can climb full time, every day of their lives, eight hours a day – either on the rock or on a climbing wall. They have to do this because the climbs that remain, the new Extremes and the unconquered routes, are of course much harder, the pitches more strenuous,

Dave Armstrong placing runners on Tophet Wall, Great Gable. Metal chocks (wedges) are jammed into cracks, and are attached to karabiners through which the rope passes. This 'running belay' system affords protection against a fall. (AB)

more sustained and technically very demanding. The climbers need to tap an almost untried source of energy to attempt today's E6s and E7s. If you are going to do a 100 foot, overhanging, fingertip clinging pitch, it takes a lot of dedication. And when you reach that standard, to get to the next stage requires huge effort and intensive training, perhaps for years. Climbers reach the peak of their ability at different ages, of course. Some are 'over the hill' at thirty-six, others later, not only physically, but mentally, too.

Whillance says: 'With many serious routes you accept that the climbs are well cleaned and brushed beforehand,' like the staircase of the Dorchester Hotel. 'So you have a reasonable idea of the difficulty you are likely to encounter. You have to be able to judge what you are capable of, and then to leave something in reserve. My serious routes tend to be low-angle walls (low in the sense of acute, not of height) because I happen to be particularly good at those; if you are very good at footwork you can always take some of the weight off your hands, and this gives you the chance to stop and think and make the next move. In long and continuous sections of over-hanging rock you can't rest because your arms are running out of strength, and they are your weakest part, and if you don't do things right first time, you fall off. . . .' In 1984, Whillance, 'over the hill', did an incredible forty new routes, and the titles were typical: Dead on Arrival, Coroner's Crack, Stage Fright.

'The first person who inaugurates a climb gives it a name, and a popular method is to continue that theme when naming neighbouring climbs. To-phet Wall on Great Gable, where we did Incantations for Border Television, has a theme of Hell. There are climbs on there called Brimstone, Lucifer and Supernatural. Climbers these days tend to follow music tracks they happen to like, or groups, or book and film titles. I'm doing forty new routes a year and making up the names is the hardest bloody part of the job.'

Every sport is subject to a set of rules made early in the game. Should the sport lose its vigour, its dynamism, or be hampered in some way in its natural progress by these rules, then the sport's practitioners seek to make the rules more flexible and less confining. In climbing there has always been argument for and against the use of artificial aid (mainly against) such as the use of piton and slings. In the early days the subject was endlessly discussed in pub bars and clubrooms: does heaving yourself up on an ice-axe constitute aid? What about standing on a partner's shoulders to gain height? What about plimsolls, and now chalk? The ultimate aim of the climber is simplicity – to get up the rock from the bottom to the top with a minimum of preparation and protection. In an interview with Bill Birkett in

Climber and Rambler magazine, Pete Whillance discussed the ethics of what is known as 'yo-yoing'. He and his partner Dave Armstrong decided that yo-yoing was acceptable. Yo-yoing means falling off and climbing back up again, and going up and down until you succeed in overcoming the problem and finally making your move. As the routes get harder the risks are increased and the protection necessarily becomes more systematic and technically advanced. You are bound to fall off, but you will not fall far because you have got more micronut belays embedded in the rock than almonds in a Dundee cake. You have also got friends jammed under flakes, your feet are glued to the rock with sticky boots and your fingers are as floury as a pastry-cook's. Ron Fawcett, now widely regarded as Britain's leading climber (a title he shares with Gerry Moffat), is a tall, curly haired, dark and moustached buccaneer who carries karabiners clamped between his teeth. He believes that future progress in climbing will be through the survival of the fittest. Technical innovation will, he says, come more slowly, and fitness and training are what will really count. For Fawcett and others like him, climbing is about bursting muscles and streaming sweat, body power and weight ratios and progressively harder routes which the man with the greatest arm-stretch will win.

In a way, the entire rock-climbing ethic is self-defeating: as routes get harder, as they must, risk is increased in proportion. This not only deters many climbers but threatens the progress of those who dare. To make exceptionally hard moves you not only have to train relentlessly, you also have to ensure adequate protection to carry them out. Thus the protection gets more complex until you are trapped like a fly in a web of belays and ropes – so the aim of retaining freedom and simplicity is frustrated. The rock wins because rock-climbers are purists and idealists – essentially *free* climbers. But the freedom of climbing seems to be curtailed by the restrictions of yo-yoing and advanced protection. The fluidity of movement, so rewarding and encouraging, becomes inhibited and arrested. After climbing the West Face of the Dru, Whillans wrote: 'I felt that surge of exhilaration and strength which means good climbing form. This was the life: no dodging out of the way of stray rocks and ice, no chancy moves on bad rock; just us with all our skill against formidable but reliable opposition. We thrived on technical difficulties, moving confidently and quickly, enjoying every foot of the climb.' Perhaps, in the final analysis, it is better to go back to the v-diffs and VS's after all, than towards the frontiers of E8 6c. But, as I have said before, climbing, like all things in life, is progressive and cannot retreat. It may be stagnant for a period, but it will eventually move forward to conquer

Soloing on Goat Crag, Borrowdale. To solo means to climb alone and without a rope, which one climber described as 'a very unforgiving sport'. (AB)

A really 'necky' route such as the Whillance/Armstrong Incantations may have to wait a long time before it is repeated by other climbers. (BT)

Whillance and Armstrong surveying the route Incantations on Tophet Wall, Great Gable, a hard and challenging climb typical of Whillance's style. (CB) the unconquerable.

Early in 1983, Whillance and Armstrong surveyed a possible new and very hard route on Tophet Wall, Great Gable, and adjacent to an existing climb called Tophet Grooves. To discover an unclimbed route up Gable is rather like trying to create a fresh advertising approach to detergents or breakfast cereals. The potential climb, later to be known as Incantations (E5/6), has a relatively easy first pitch (VS) of seventy to eighty feet, but the remaining three pitches were daunting. They failed on their first two attempts, mainly because the weather was too cold, and you cannot, with frozen fingers, tackle a climb that demands a virtuoso performance. A year later, and on a warm summer evening, the two climbers abseiled down Tophet Wall and brushed up the rock as a barber brushes loose hairs from his client's shoulders. The route would 'go'. they concluded, if they could find a suitable place for a peg runner (piton and sling) for protection on the overhanging wall of the crux pitch. Placing a peg during route inspection has sometimes been thought unethical but if pre-placing a runner makes all the difference between success and failure (and life and death), and is not used to pull up on or to stand on, then the act is permissible. 'People have been doing it for years.' says Whillance, 'and I cannot think of any climber remotely bothered by it. In fact, I was opposed to pre-placing and was perhaps the last to be converted.'

The second pitch of the climb is 130 feet, half of which is continuously overhanging wall and graded 6b for strenuousness and technical difficulty. The remainder of the climb goes up a thin crack in 60 feet of severely over-hanging wall. It is at this point that Whillance abseiled down and saw there was only one possible place for a peg runner – a position that was almost out of reach – but he had no option and had to rely on Dave Armstrong's long arms and extra height. Had he come off, he would have fallen well over a hundred feet hitting a slab *en route*. When on the actual climb, Armstrong found that the peg was almost beyond his reach, and had to make a desperate lunge to clip a karabiner on the runner. This is why Incantations is an E6 6b climb – there is high risk with limited protection and hard climbing. The top section of the climb goes up a V-groove to a final fifty feet and the top.

There are still a lot of very hard and taxing climbs to do in the Lake District. There is, for example, a line on Scafell, on the East Buttress, which awaits a super climber cast in the mould of Livesey or Whillance. Of course, since it has not been climbed it has not yet been named. Perhaps End of Story would be a suitable title.

Bibliography

Don Whillans. Portrait of a mountaineer. Don Whillans & Alick Ormerod. Heinemann 1971.

Space Below My Feet. Gwen Moffat. Hodder & Stoughton 1961.

The First Tigers. Alan Hankinson. Melbecks Books 1984. First pub. J.M. Dent 1972.

Lakeland's Pioneer Rock Climbers. Herbert and Mary Jackson. The Dalesman Pub. Co. 1980.

Crag and Hound in Lakeland. C.E. Benson. Hurst & Blackett 1902.

Peaks, Passes & Glaciers. John Ball (Ed). Longman, Green 1860.

Rock Climbing in the English Lake District. O.G. Jones. George Abraham & Sons 1900.

A History of British Mountaineering. Robert Irving. Batsford 1955.

British Crags and Climbers. Edward Pyatt & Wilfrid Noyce. Dennis Dobson 1952.

Enjoy your Rock Climbing. Anthony Greenbank. Pelham Books 1976.

Rock Climbing. Arthur Clark and Ian Price. Barrie & Jenkins 1979.

Women on the Rope. Cicely Williams. Allen & Unwin 1973.

Alpine Heights and British Crags. George Abraham. Methuen 1919.

Rock Climbing in Britain. Jeremiah Wright. Nicholas Kaye 1958.

Mountaineering. The All England Series. Claude Wilson. Geo. Bell 1893.

Freeman of the Hills. A.H. Griffin. Robert Hale 1978.

Lakeland's Greatest Pioneers. Bill Birkett. Robert Hale 1983.

The Next Horizon. Chris Bonington. Victor Gollancz 1973.

I Chose to Climb. Chris Bonington. Victor Gollancz 1966.

Climber and Fellwalker in Lakeland. Frank Monkhouse and Joe Williams. David & Charles 1972.

The True Blue. Michael Alexander. Rupert Hart-Davis 1957.

Rock Climbing in the Lake District. Geoff Cram, Chris Eilbeck, Ian Roper. Constable 1975.

The Lakes to Tyneside. About Britain Series No 10. Sid Chaplin. Collins 1951.

Journey Through Britain. John Hillaby. Paladin 1970.

The Fell & Rock Climbing Club Guides. Pub. F&RCC.

Technical Notes

Bill Peascod

The climb   Eagle Front, Eagle Crag, Buttermere
First ascent by   Bill Peascod and Bert Beck
Date   June 1940
Grade   VS
Gear used
Rope   100 foot hemp rope
Protection   One hemp sling, one karabiner
Footwear   Woolworth gym shoes
Major first ascents
Lakes
Eagle Front, VS, Eagle Crag, Buttermere;   Dexter Wall, VS, Grey Crag, Buttermere;   Y Gully, VS, Haystacks, Buttermere; Cleopatra, VS, Buckstone How, Buttermere;   Jezebel, VS, Miner's Crag, Buttermere;   Delilah, VS, High Crag, Buttermere;   Eve, VS, Shepherd's Crag, Borrowdale.

Elsewhere in UK
Minus Two Gully, VS, Ben Nevis

Don Whillans

The climb   Dovedale Groove, Dove Crag, Dovedale
First ascent   Don Whillans, Joe Brown (leading through) and Don Cowan
Date   4 May 1953
Original grade   Very severe, with one point of aid
Grade   E1

Gear used
Rope   One hundred and twenty foot hawser lay full weight rope
Protection   A variety of line and three quarter weight slings. Chock stones picked up at bottom of crag
Footwear   Gym shoes

Major first ascents
Lakes
Triermain Eliminate, Castle Rock, Thirlmere with Joe Brown, E2, 1953; Girdle Traverse, Dierbield Crag, with Ron Moseley, E2, 1953; Trinity, East Buttress, Scafell, with Sutherland, HVS; Extol, Dove Crag, Dovedale, with Colin Mortlock, E2, 1960.
Elsewhere in UK
Cemetry Gates, Dinas Cromlech, North Wales, with Joe Brown, HVS, 1951; The Sloth, The Roaches, Staffs, with Brown, VS, 1952; Sassenach, Carn Dearg Buttress, Ben Nevis, with Brown, HVS, 1954; Erosion Groove Direct, Carreg Wasted, North Wales, with Brown, E1, 1955; Slanting Slab, Clogwyn dur Arddu, North Wales, with Betts, E2, 3 pts aid, 1955; Sceptre, Clogwyn dur Arduu, with Betts, HVS, 1955; Great Crack, Froggatt, Derbyshire, with party, HVS, 1955; Cromlech Girdle, Dinas Cromlech with Brown, E2 with 3 pts aid, 1956; Centurion, Carn Dearg Buttress, Ben Nevis with Bob Downes, HVS, 1956; The Shield, Carn Dearg Buttress, with Bob Downes, HVS, 1956; Grond, Dinas Cromlech with party, E2, 1958; Sentinal Crack, Chatsworth, with Sutcliffe, E3, 6A, 1959.
Abroad
West Face, Aiguille de Blaitiere, Chamonix with Brown, 1954; Central Pillar Freney, Mont Blanc, with Bonington, Clough and Djuglosz, 1961; Aiguille Poincenot, Patagonia, with Cochrane, 1962; Central Tower Paine, Patagonia, with Bonington, 1963; Annapurna South Face, Nepal, with Haston, 1970.

Chris Bonington

The climb Holy Ghost, East Buttress of Scafell
First ascent by Chris Bonington and Mike Thompson
Date April 1965
Original grade Extremely severe
Grade E2

Gear used
Rope Two one hundred and fifty foot hawser lay three quarter weight ropes
Protection A variety of line and three quarter weight slings threaded with drilled out Whitworth nuts of different sizes, plus a hammer and small piton selection.
Footwear P.A.s

Major first ascents
Lakes
The Medlar, Raven Crag, Thirlmere, with Martin Boysen leading through, and Mike Thompson, 3 pts aid, today E3, 1964; Totalitarian, Raven Crag, Thirlmere with Mike Thompson, E1, 1964; The White Wizard, Central Buttress, Scafell with Nick Estcourt 5 pts aid, today E3, 1971.
Elsewhere in UK
Mercavity, Main Wall, Avon Gorge, with Geoff Francis, HVS, 1955; Malpractice, Main Wall, Avon gorge, with Mike Thompson, VS, 1956; Malbogies, Main Wall,

Avon Gorge with Geoff Francis and Henry Rogers, VS, 1957; Girdle Traverse, Coire Mhic Fhearchar, with Tom Patey, S, 1960; King Cobra, Correachen Ruadha Face, Skye, Tom Patey, VS, 1960; Coronation Street, Cheddar Gorge, with Tony Greenbank and John Cleare, with one point of aid, E1, 1965; Original Route, Old Man of Hoy, with Tom Patey and Rusty Bailey, HVS, 1966.
Abroad
Annapurna II, (26,041 ft.) with Dick Grant, 1960; Nuptse, (25,850 ft.) with Les Brown, Jim Swallow and Sherpa Ang Pema, 1961; Central Pillar of Freney, Mont Blanc with Don Whillans, Ian Clough and Jan Djuglosz, 1961; Central Tower of Paine in Patagonia, with Don Whillans, 1963; Right Hand Pillar of Brouillard on Mont Blanc with Rusty Baillie, Brian Robertson and John Harlin, 1965; Annapurna South Face, Leader, 1970; Brammah (21,036 ft.) in Kishtwar with Nick Estcourt, 1973; Changabang (22,520 ft.) in the Garhwal Himalaya with Martin Boysen, Dougal Haston, Balwant Sandhu, Doug Scott and Sherpa Tenzing, 1974; Everest South West Face, leader, 1975; The Ogre, (23,900 ft.) Karakoram, with Doug Scott, 1977; Kongur, (25,325 ft.) Sinkiang with Peter Boardman, Al Rouse and Joe Tasker, 1981; Shivling West Summit, (21,330 ft.) in the Gangotri, with Jim Fotheringham, 1983.

Pete Livesey

The climb   Footless Crow, Goat Crag, Borrowdale
First ascent   Pete Livesey
Date   April, 1974
Grade   E5

Gear used
Rope   Two 9 mm Kernmantl ropes
Protection   20 karabiners, clog nuts (wedges) on wire, moac wedges on rope, chuinard eccentrics on rope, three tape and three rope slings. Swami belt
Footwear and clothing   EB shoes, lightweight stretchable polar suit

Major first ascents
Lakes
Footless Crow, E5, Goat Crag, Borrowdale; Bitter Oasis, E3, Goat Crag, Borrowdale; Fine Time E3, Raven Crag, Langdale; Longhair, E3, White Ghyll, Langdale; Lost Horizons, Scafell; Das Kapital, E5, Raven Crag, Thirlmere.
Elsewhere in UK
Wellington Crack, Cow & Calf, Ilkley; Downhill Racer, Froggat Edge, Derwent Valley; Face Route, Gordale Scar; Jenny Wren, Gordale Scar; Deliverance, Gordale Scar; Bastile, High Tor, Matlock; Golden Mile, Chee Tor, Buxton; Central Wall, Kilnsey Crag; Claws, Kilnsey Crag; Doubting Thomas, Malham Cove; Zero, Suicide Wall, CWm Idwal; Great Wall, E4, Craig y Forwyn, Snowdonia; Right Wall, E5, Dinas Cromlech; Wailing Wall, E4, Craig y Lyn; Fingerlicker, E4, Craig Pant Ifan; West Face Route, The Great Zawn, Cornwall; Fool's Lode, E5, Great Zawn; Last Leviathan, Pentyre Head, North Cornwall.

First Free ascents, USA
Lightweights don't Scream, Sierra Nevada, California;   Mortician, Carbon Wall, and North-West Face of Sentinel Rock, all in Yosemite.

Jill Lawrence & Gill Price

The climb   Empire, Raven Crag, Thirlmere
Date   August 1984 (first ascent by K. Myhill & K. Jones (var) Sept. 1973
Grade   E3
Gear used
Rope   Two 9 mm Kermantl ropes
Protection   25 clog karabiners each; they shared: set of 9 rock wedges on wire, chuinard hexagonal nuts on rope, set of friends, 3 short tape slings; extenders (tie-off 4-inch sewn tape slings with karabiners prevents climbing rope lifting the nuts out of the cracks). Each carried a chalk bag
Footwear and clothing   Fire's sticky boots, Whillans harness

Jill Lawrence's major climbs
Lakes
Empire, E3, Raven Crag, Thirlmere; Bitter Oasis, E3, Goat Crag, Borrow-dale; Vertigo, E2, Black Crag, Borrowdale; Prana, E3, Black Crag, Borrow-dale; White Wizard, Scafell.
Elsewhere in UK
Right Wall, E5, Dinas Cromlech; Resurrection, E4, Dinas Cromlech; Zukator, E4, Craig Bwlch y Moch; Zangorilla, E3, Carreg Wastad, Llanberis; Fingerlicker, E4, Craig Pant Ifan; Tux, Gogarth.

Gill Price's major climbs
Lakes   Prana, E3, Black Crag, Borrowdale; Nagasaki Grooves, E4, Greatend Crag, Borrowdale; Empire, E3, Raven Crag, Thirlmere; White Wizard, Scafell.
Elsewhere in UK
Resurrection, E4, Dinas Cromlech, Wales; Left Wall, E3, Dinas Cromlech, Wales; Zukator, E4, Craig Bwlch y Moch, Tremadog; Venom, E3, Craig Bwlch y Moch, Tremadog; Atomic Finger Flake, E4, Craig Bwlch y Moch, Trema-dog; Manor Park, E3, Upper Tier, Gogarth, Anglesea; The Strand, ES, Upper Tier, Gogarth, Anglesea; Aardvark, E2, Main Cliff, Gogarth; Big Groove, ES, Main Cliff, Gogarth.

Pete Whillance

The climb   Incantations, Tophet Wall, Great Gable
First ascent by   Pete Whillance and Dave Armstrong
Date   August, 1984
Grade   E6

Gear used
Rope   Two 9 mm Kernmantle ropes

Protection   RP's (tiny brass nuts) 2 sets; 2 sets rocks; set of chuinard small stoppers (all the foregoing on wire). No 1 and No 2 friends. Set of lightweight, hollow karabiners known as quickdrawers; 14 short slings. Chalk

Footwear and clothing   Pair of Fire's (sticky boots), Whillans' harness, track suit trousers and T-shirt

Major first ascents

Lakes

Take it to the Limit E5, Deer Bield Crag, Langdale;   Stagefright E5, Hedge Close Quarry;   Incantations, E6, Tophet Wall, Great Gable;   Coroner's Crack,   Eagle Crag, Borrowdale;   Dead on Arrival,   Eagle Crag, Borrowdale.

Elsewhere in UK

Midsummer Night's Dream, E5, Cloggy (Clogwyn d'ur Arddu), Snowdonia;   Energy Crisis E4, Upper Tier, Gogarth, Anglesea;   Long Run, E5, North Stack area, Anglesea;   White Heat, E5, White Tower, Pembroke;   Tangerine Dream, E4, St. Govan's Head, Pembroke;   Godspell, E4, Black Church Cliff, Bude;   Culm Dancing, Exmansworthy, Devon;   Risk Business, E5, Glencoe, Scotland;   Naked Ape E6, Cairngorms;   Run of the Arrow, Cairngorms;   Agrippa, Ben Nevis;   Edge of Extinction, The Brack, Arrocher.

Index